SIR ROBERT TAYLOR

From Rococo to Neoclassicism

GENIUS OF ARCHITECTURE
Series editors:
JOHN HARRIS and MARCUS BINNEY

SIR ROBERT TAYLOR

From Rococo to Neoclassicism

MARCUS BINNEY

London
GEORGE ALLEN & UNWIN
Boston   Sydney

George Allen & Unwin (Publishers) Ltd,
40 Museum Street, London WC1A 1LU, UK

George Allen & Unwin (Publishers) Ltd,
Park Lane, Hemel Hempstead, Herts HP2 4TE, UK

Allen & Unwin Inc.,
9 Winchester Terrace, Winchester, Mass 01890, USA

George Allen & Unwin Australia Pty Ltd.,
8 Napier Street, North Sydney, NSW 2060, Australia

First published in 1984

British Library Cataloguing in Publication Data

Binney, Marcus
    Sir Robert Taylor 1714–1788.—(Genius
    of architecture; 4)
    1. Taylor, *Sir* Robert, *1714–1788*
    I. Title   II. Series
    720′.92′4   NA997.T3/
    ISBN 0-04-720028-6
    ISBN 0-04-720031-6 Pbk

Set in 11 on 13 point Sabon by Computape (Pickering) Ltd,
North Yorkshire
and printed in Great Britain by
William Clowes Limited, Beccles and London

Contents

To the Vannecks

List of illustrations

Acknowledgments

This book is the result of a lucky choice of subject for my BA thesis at Cambridge in 1966 – a choice I owe to a suggestion of Walter Ison's. No one had really worked on Taylor before and I had an open field – and I little suspected at the time that Sir Robert was to lead me both to a job as architectural writer at *Country Life* and to the purchase of one of his buildings Barlaston Hall (and all its problems) for the princely sum of £1. John Harris, co-editor of this series, fired me with innumerable leads, Howard Colvin generously and patiently answered a long stream of questions. Edmund Esdaile bombarded me with thoughts and ideas about Taylor's early life and sculpture.

Since 1966 I have pursued my work on Taylor principally through a series of articles in *Country Life*, material which the editor, Michael Wright, has kindly allowed me to incorporate here. To Sophie Andreae, fellow-director of the Barlaston Hall Trust, who has taken on the main work of organising and supervising the repairs I owe a special debt. To my wife Anne are due the thanks all authors must express for their wife's encouragement and forbearance and in this case also for typing a considerable part of the manuscript.

Among those who own or look after Taylor's buildings I offer particular thanks to Mr and Mrs Maurice Ash at Sharpham, Mr Fred Hauptführer at Asgill House, Mrs Norah King who was for many years Lord Verulam's secretary at Gorhambury and Mr and Mrs David Wheeler formerly at Heveningham.

In addition I wish to acknowledge help of many different kinds from Adrian Allan; Ashley Barker; Peter Bezodis; Miss Nancy Briggs of the Essex Record Office; Marc Cameron-Swan; Lord Carrington; Nicholas Cooper; John Cornforth; Alan George; Celia de la Hey; W. M. T. Fowle; Mark Girouard; Andor Gomme; John Greenacombe; Eileen Harris; Peter Hodson; Simon Houfe; Lord and Lady Huntingfield; Ruth Hutcheson;

Alastair Laing; David Lloyd; Calder Loth; Kit Martin; Emma Milne; J. Mordaunt Crook; Barry Morgan; Susan Moore; P.E. Morris; Mrs A.E.B. Owen; Alistair Rowan; the late Lord Spencer; Mrs Statham of the Suffolk Record Office; Miss Dorothy Stroud; Sir John Summerson; Reginald Thompson; B. Trainor of the Public Record Office of Northern Ireland; David Watkin; Roger White; J. St A. Warde.

Over the years I have visited and corresponded with numerous public libraries and county record offices; the source material they have provided is described in the notes.

I could have written a longer book on Taylor but have chosen this series partly because it means a book considerably cheaper than the standard full-scale monograph and partly because I am sure that in the next few years more documentation about Taylor will appear. The bicentenary of Taylor's death will I hope provide the opportunity for a further examination of his work. Taylor's sculpture is only touched briefly here but is shortly to receive a fuller consideration by Malcolm Baker in the catalogue of the exhibition on English Rococo to be held at the Victoria and Albert Museum in the spring of 1984.

Photographic acknowledgments

Ashmolean Museum, Oxford 18; Governor & Company of the Bank of England 8, 9, 12, 13, 14; Country Life 4, 5, 6, 25, 29, 30, 41, 44, 47, 52, 53, 54, 55, 56, 57, 58, 72, 74, 75, 80, 81; Courtauld Institute of Art 2, 3, 7, 10, 11, 15, 16, 17, 21, 23, 24, 32, 33, 39, 40, 45, 46, 49, 50, 51, 79; Christopher Dalton 34, 35, 36, 38; Greater London Council 42, 43, 64, 65, 66, 67, 68, 69, 70, 71, 73, 76, 77, 78; National Monuments Record 26, 27, 28, 31, 63; National Portrait Gallery 1; Save Britain's Heritage 34, 37; Taylor Institution 59, 60, 61, 62.

Introduction

Sir Robert Taylor's memorial in Poets' Corner in Westminster Abbey proudly proclaims that 'his works entitle him to a distinguished rank in the first class of British architect'. Though the memorial tablet is restrained it is conspicuously placed, two along from David Garrick, two above James Wyatt. Sir William Chambers, by contrast, is on the floor, half hidden by pews. How did Taylor achieve so prominent a placing? Was it by worldly success, by influential friends, or simply by dying at the right moment when Poets' Corner was of recent creation and there was still space on the walls for successful practitioners of all the arts?

John Nash, Taylor's most famous pupil, was not very flattering about his former master. Taylor, he told Farington on 5 November 1821, 'had no skill in drawing but made shift to get on. He went to Rome which might give him more pretension in his profession.'[1]

By contrast, C. R. Cockerell, whose father, S. P. Cockerell, had been another of Taylor's pupils, admired Taylor's subtle planning and in his Royal Academy lectures praised his Bank of England and Bank Buildings.[2] Soane, he told Farington in 1807, 'had displayed some understanding' at the Bank of England 'as by pulling down that which Sir Robert had built it could no longer be a reproach to him by its contrasts to all the bad taste which he Soane had manifested in every other part'.[3]

Horace Walpole, who was responsible for Taylor's obituary in the *Gentleman's Magazine*, had a high opinion of his talents: 'he seems from the beginning to have been of those independent original powers which are reciprocally self-formed and self-forming'.[4] Thirty years later the *Gentleman's Magazine* was not so kind, referring cuttingly to Taylor's 'two high houses on the south side of Lincoln's Inn Fields and many other ungraceful piles'.[5] James Fergusson in his *History of Modern Styles* (1862) thought Taylor had done little to justify the patronage bestowed on him.

In this century Taylor has suffered from what I would term the linear school of architectural history, which has given the laurels to innovation much more than accomplishment. Taylor has been cast as a second-generation Palladian, a follower rather than an inventor. There is a certain irony here for in a way the first generation of English Palladians – notably Colen Campbell and Lord Burlington (as well as Inigo Jones before them) – were much more concerned with following precedents and models than Taylor was. Sir John Summerson in his pioneering monograph on John Nash, first published in 1935, tried to show that Taylor was not a dull architect, but nonetheless summarised him in his Pelican *History of Architecture in Britain 1530–1830* as 'a Palladian with eclectic proclivities which may or may not mean that, in his later years he would have relied on 'ghosts'.[6] The Penguin *Dictionary of Architecture* (1966) dismissed him as 'conservative and uninspired, but highly competent, and worthily carrying on the Neo-Palladian tradition of Burlington and Kent'.[7] Nor did Taylor fare well in the early volumes on the *Building of England*. Ian Nairn, in the first edition of his provocative and caustic volume on Surrey, even suggested that because Taylor's Thorncroft was so dull Asgill, one of Taylor's best known works, must be by a pupil. Hardest of all was H. R. Steele in his memorial volume on *The Old Bank of England* (1930). Taylor, he says, 'borrowed shamelessly from all sources in designing his contributions to the Bank'.[8]

In this century Taylor fared better with what might be termed the dilettante (in the best sense of the word) school of architectural writers. Sir Albert Richardson in his *Monumental Classic Architecture in Great Britain and Ireland* (1914) astutely observed that 'from the standpoint of monumental design his important architectural works were in marked contrast to those of many of his contemporaries, being distinguished by simplicity of composition and almost Spartan severity in the selection of enrichments'.[9] Sacheverell Sitwell in his *British Architects and Craftsmen* (1945) noted that Taylor's works were 'easily recognisable by certain mannerisms' and noted 'at times, a fantasy that reminds one of the interiors of certain churches in Turin and must derive from his experiences in Italy ... Coming to architecture, out of sculpture, Taylor was not entirely ordinary in his approach, but was an amateur, not in technique, but in the first conception'.[10] Both Richardson and Sitwell were constrained in their appreciation of Taylor, as were other contemporaries, by focusing discussion on a small group of works, the Bank of England, Ely House in Dover Street, Stone Buildings in Lincoln's Inn and Heveningham, which do not reveal Taylor's full range as an architect.

For quite apart from adverse critical comment one reason why Taylor's name fell into near obscurity was that so much of his work had disappeared or simply been forgotten. Thomas Hardwick in a much-quoted remark in his manuscript memoir of Sir William Chambers observed that Taylor and James Paine 'nearly divided the practice of the profession between them for they had few competitors till Mr Robert Adam entered the lists'.[11] Yet until recently the list of Taylor's works has been much shorter than this would suggest.

Most of Taylor's London works have been demolished – notably the two remarkable rococo houses in Lincoln's Inn Fields and Grafton House in Piccadilly and his own house in Spring Gardens, which Walpole thought so pretty that 'foreigners should see it'.[12] Against this is the discovery of documentary evidence that the fine group of houses at 3–6 Grafton Street are by Taylor, though they are only survivors of a group of at least fourteen.

Among Taylor's country houses Purbrook in Hampshire and Coptfold in Essex were demolished in the nineteenth century; Porter's Lodge in Hertfordshire has been engulfed in later buildings. Three of his most important villas – Barlaston, Danson and Harleyford – all fell into a very poor state of repair in the 1960s and 1970s. Among his country houses only Heveningham was sufficiently complete to warrant a chapter in one of Christoper Hussey's trilogy on Georgian county houses, while only one of Taylor's houses, Asgill, was illustrated in *Vitruvius Britannicus*, the great contemporary showcase of Palladian architecture.

Many eighteenth-century architects are known best by their public commissions. Taylor has suffered severely from the loss of his one major public work, as Howard Colvin observes in his *Dictionary of British Architects 1600–1840* (1978): 'But for the unfortunate destruction of nearly all his work at the Bank of England he would have been better known as a major English classical architect.'

The obscurity surrounding Taylor has been deepened by a remarkable lack of drawings and papers. The reassessment and renewed appreciation of many eighteenth-century architects in recent years has rested in considerable part on the collections of architectural drawings of the Royal Institute of British Architects, the Soane Museum and the Victoria and Albert Museum. By contrast the only sizeable groups of Taylor's drawings to survive are three volumes in the Taylor Institution at Oxford, one of designs for monuments, a second of drawings of rococo chimney-pieces and a third on 'Problems in Geometry and Mensuration with Diagrams'.

This is as tragic as it is perplexing, for *The World* of 7 November 1788 notes that 'His drawings were left highly finished, and arranged in perfect series'. Their disappearance may be connected with the long dispute over Taylor's will, and it may be that they will suddenly reappear – as some of Taylor's architectural books did recently at the Taylorian.[13] As it is, a few clusters of drawings have come to light among estate papers and other records, for example for a room at Trewithen in Cornwall, for Maidenhead Bridge, and for the church at Long Ditton and the spire at St Peter's Wallingford, but in all they amount to less than two dozen.

Taylor, unlike Adam, Chambers and Paine, never published an architectural treatise or corpus of his own works. However, after his death his son Michelangelo commissioned a set of thirty-two aquatints of Taylor's principal works by Thomas Malton junior, which were published in 1790–2.[14] These, alas, are very rare, perhaps because they were not offered on general sale, but simply presented to friends and colleagues.

Correspondence and documents are equally lacking apart from Walpole's obituary and a series of articles and reports published in the daily newspaper *The World* in 1787 and 1788.[15] In addition, of course, there is the documentation associated with the various buildings themselves, though this too is far from copious in most cases.

Fortunately, Taylor's work bears very strong and clear hallmarks which provide a firm basis for building up an impressive corpus of work. Of course numerous contemporaries use a stylistic vocabulary similar to Taylor's, but the combinations of certain features that recur throughout his work as well as his very distinctive planning together form a basis for firm and confident attributions, reinforced by the close connections between various groups of patrons.

In his domestic buildings – town houses, villas and all but the largest country houses – Taylor is astylar in his treatment of elevations (Plate 45). He uses what can be conveniently called the House of Raphael formula which is the basis of all Palladian design – that is a basement (which may be a ground floor) carrying a *piano nobile* or principal floor and a lower floor of bedrooms above. Taylor however invariably eschews the use of an order of columns or pilasters over the basement. In sharp contrast to the first generation of Palladian villas in England such as Chiswick, Mereworth and Stourhead, none of his villas have porticoes, either projecting or applied. They may have pediments, and certainly a cornice, but never a full entablature and never columns. Basements were plain or rusticated, and he made great play with vermiculated rustication around doors and arches – vermiculation being technically an imitation of worm tracks. The same is true of London houses – for example the handsome ashlar front of Ely House in Dover Street (Plate 79).

In his villas Taylor also made great play with projecting bays, both canted and three-sided bays, and large semi-elliptical bows. Thus he broke radically from the first generation of Palladian villas which were square or rectangular in plan (Plate 33).

Whereas Robert Adam's highly adventurous plans for country houses were rarely put into practice, Taylor succeeded, with all his principal villas, in persuading patrons to accept broken plans and highly varied elevations. It may be that his patrons being largely men of business not requiring very large houses responded more positively to the sense of show Taylor's designs provided in combination with compactness and austerity. Taylor's use of bays also introduced extra light and provided wider views from within, and by varying the height of the projecting bays (those at the sides usually rise only to the *piano nobile*, those at the back the full height of the house) he produced that sense of movement in elevations which Adam wrote so eloquently of in his *Essay on Architecture*.[16]

The use of projecting bays provided opportunities for creating rooms of unusual shape within — not just rooms with large bows on the longer wall, but circular, octagonal and D-shaped rooms, as well as pairs of ovals fitted side by side within an octagonal core.

A second recurrent feature of Taylor's buildings is the cantilevered staircase, usually in stone, though in early villas, like Harleyford and Barlaston, in wood (Plate 38). Taylor's practice, following Inigo Jones's famous tulip stair at Greenwich over a century earlier, was to cut away the underside of the treads to create an effect of great lightness. In both town and country houses Taylor tended to place staircases in the centre of the house, lighting them from above rather than from the side by means of circular and oval domes (Plate 74). The central position of the staircase hall and the landings above helped eliminate the need for corridors: most rooms opened directly onto the staircase hall (or the adjoining front hall) and the landings.

Almost all Taylor's buildings have very extensive basements which ensured that they were well aired and free of rising damp. In earlier country houses vaulted basements were often restricted to an area of cellars under part of the house. Taylor's villas have both the traditional Palladian basement beneath the *piano nobile* and usually a sub-basement. The sub-basements are surrounded by a submerged dry brick walk, usually running right round the house. The London houses are similar: in addition to the usual basement approached by steps in the front area (what is euphemistically termed a lower ground floor today) there is a second sub-basement.

A motif that occurs throughout Taylor's career is the arcade resting on columns placed at one or both ends of the room (Plate 13). Cockerell noted this in a Royal Academy Lecture in 1845,[17] while describing the Court Room at the Bank of England: 'you enter the room by lateral corridors from whence the proportion of the room is entirely enjoyed as it was from an external point of view.' A variant of this is his use of the Palladian arch motif at one end of the room, resting on columns and serving sometimes as a recess for a bed. Taylor also made great play with cross-vaulting. His rare corridors are often roofed in this way, as are vestibules or small cabinets. The arches between the cross-vaults are usually inset with a guilloche pattern.

Other motifs naturally evolve during his career. One signature to the early works, like 35 Lincoln's Inn Fields and Harleyford, is the use of octagonal glazing in the windows – matched sometimes by octagonal panels in the doors and shutters (Plates 26 and 30), and, as at Barlaston, in the stone paving of the hall and the glass doors of the library bookcases. The octagonal glazing is a feature of Taylor's first rococo phase in the 1750s, and with it go a series of highly decorative rococo chimney-pieces, several very close to his designs for chimney-pieces in the Taylor Institution.

In the 1760s Taylor is more classical and by the end of the decade his interior decoration is evolving parallel with Robert Adam. Like Chambers and Paine he adhered to Rome, and the Greek introductions of Stuart and Revett did not touch him.

Taylor made frequent use of Venetian windows. At 35 Lincoln's Inn Fields they appear both outside (Plate 65) and inside (Plate 70), while two of the 1750s villas, Coptfold and Barlaston, have large Venetian arches over the canted bays at the side of the house (Plates 32 and 35). In both cases the central arch is enclosed by an outer arch in the manner of those on the garden front of Lord Burlington's Chiswick House. The motif appears again at the Bank of England in the 1760s where the west quadrangle (Plate 15) is surrounded by Venetian windows. Here Taylor introduced a new lightness by glazing in the outer arch – an idea that evidently came to him while working out the design – an early, more rococo drawing for the Court Room (Plate 12) shows a solid outer arch.

In the course of his career Taylor took Palladianism a long way down the road to neo-Classicism. At Purbrook House he introduced what is almost certainly the earliest re-creation of a Roman atrium in England (Plate 51) which in plan has close parallels with the house of Castor and Pollux at Herculaneum which was being excavated in the 1750s.

At Sharpham (Plate 53) the elegant but austere front, in exquisite ashlar, shows that preoccupation with perfection of materials that was to be a hallmark of the Greek Revival. Inside Sharpham demonstrates a neo-Classical concern with simple geometric volumes and spatial relationships. Here, as at Purbrook, hall and staircase flow directly into one another with no doors to separate them (Plate 54). The purest of these volumes is undoubtedly the great staircase at Sharpham with the great oval dome rising directly from the walls (Plate 56) – an architectural *tour-de-force* deserving comparison with Gondouin's famous semi-circular amphitheatre at the Ecole de Chirurgie in Paris (1769–74).

Taylor's development towards neo-Classicism is most evident in his very last works – particularly the Reduced Annuity Office at the Bank of England, completed in 1787 (Plate 16). Here the shallow segmental arches supporting a sidelit dome directly anticipate the brilliant and original work of Sir John Soane, Taylor's successor as architect to the Bank. Taylor also intended a series of such domes at the Guildhall in Salisbury, as Malton's plan makes clear (Plate 24), though his pupil William Pilkington modified Taylor's plans in execution. The Guildhall plan also shows Taylor using shallow cross-vaulted ceilings – another favourite motif of Soane – carried on shallow segmental arches.

In his decoration Taylor naturally becomes steadily more Classical, and his plasterwork of the 1770s is very much influenced by Robert Adam. However one motif which is very much his own is the plaster roundel with Classical figures in relief. This appears for example at 4 Grafton Street (Plate 75) and at Purbrook (Plate 51).

Many of these features – the octagonal glazing, the canted bays, and vermiculated rustication – are of course used by Taylor's contemporaries. However his vocabulary and his planning is I believe sufficiently consistent and distinct to set his work apart and make it clearly identifiable on stylistic grounds. Obviously there is a temptation whenever a building or a plan with a canted bay appears to wonder if it might be a new work by Taylor. Over the last seventeen years I have looked at many buildings and plans in this light – Stone House, Lewisham, Stover House, Devon, Culham Court, Berkshire are just three examples of buildings with Taylorian features which nonetheless did not seem to me to be by Taylor.

In several of these cases documentation has appeared to suggest they are by other architects. However it is equally clear that more verifiable works by Taylor will come to light — unexecuted, demolished and one hopes still surviving, and the principal purpose of this book is to establish a clear and well-documented *oeuvre* which will form a secure basis for adding to the lists of Taylor's works in the future.

1 Life

To some writers the only colourful moment in Taylor's career was provided by his father who reputedly died a virtual bankrupt leaving his son penniless. Walpole tells us that the elder Taylor, 'like Devall in the present day, got a vast deal of money; but again, unlike him altogether he could not keep what he got. When life was less gaudy than it is now and when the elegant indulgences of it were rare, old Taylor the mason enjoyed them all. He revelled at a villa in Essex; and as a villa is imperfect without a coach ... old Taylor drove a coach and four.'[1]

According to Walpole, the elder Robert Taylor (c. 1690–1742) was 'the great stone-mason of his time'.[2] He had been apprenticed under Richard Garbut, 'citizen and mason', and became free in 1712. He worked principally as a statuary but carried out decorative work and on occasion acted as mason-architect. His masterpiece as a sculptor is the magnificent monument to Thomas Deacon in Peterborough Cathedral (1721). In 1724 he received £40 for a chimney-piece at Stourhead costing £40, and in 1732 provided one for Masons' Hall. For the Grocers' Company he was carrying out decorative carving in 1735–6. From 1725 to 1739 Taylor was mason to the Royal College of Physicians and was responsible for much of the building at St Bartholomew's Hospital between 1728 and 1740, while in 1738 he was jointly involved in securing the contracts for masons', bricklayers' and carpenters' work at the Mansion House.[3]

Walpole says the younger Robert Taylor got nothing from his father 'excepting some common schooling, a fee, when he went pupil to Sir Henry Cheere, and just enough money to travel on a plan of frugal study to Rome'.[4] Taylor was apprenticed to Sir Henry Cheere (1703–81) in 1732, at the age of eighteen (not fourteen as is sometimes suggested), for the considerable fee of

£105,[5] when Cheere himself was quite a young man. His visit to Rome was cut short by his father's death in early October 1742.[6] He tried, Walpole relates, 'to hurry home; but as there was a war on the continent, as that war required certain passports' which could not be obtained, he assumed 'the apparel of a friar and joined another Franciscan, and so passed unmolested through the enemy's camp'.[7]

If Taylor returned to England late in 1742 or early in 1743 that leaves most of his early life a blank. The only documented work is a monument of 1739 to Thomas Marsh in the church at Womenswold in Kent. However, he may have been quite active even before his Italian journey and Vertue writing in 1752 refers to 'Mr Taylor the sculptor – who has infinitely polished his work beyond comparison this being another young English artist who made the tour of Italy',[8] with the implication that Taylor was practising before his Italian visit.

Walpole wrote colourfully that when Taylor came home 'he found, like Wolsey, he had nothing but his robe and integrity; that to live he must work; and to live to any good purpose, his work must be good'.[9]

The World on 8 October 1788 gives a slightly different picture of his finances: 'Out of the first twenty thousand pounds he had in the world, he gave, with the most admirable virtue, fifteen thousand between his father's debts and his brother's', while much of the remaining £5,000 he used in buying three annuities for his wife's relations. Thus, though the elder Taylor may have squandered his wealth it seems likely that his yard at least must have been in approximately working order. Certainly at least one of the older Taylor's masons continued to work for his son, John Malcot the Elder (d. 1766), who had been apprenticed to Taylor's father in 1730 and remained with him when his apprenticeship ended.[10]

Taylor soon had a large amount of work. 'In a little time', Walpole wrote, 'he did so much and so well, then when Cornwalls monument was to come, it was voted to come from Taylor.'[11] This was the monument to Captain James Cornewall (1699–1744), who was killed in action off Toulon, which stands just inside the entrance to the west cloister of Westminster Abbey (1747–55).[12] On 3 August 1744 Taylor was granted the freedom of the Masons' Company by patrimony[13] – his father had been a Warden of the Masons' Company in 1729 and 1731, and Master in 1732.[14]

In 1744 Taylor had also gained the commission for carving the pediment of the Mansion House, where his father had been working, against competition from Roubiliac and Cheere, for which he received £420.

Taylor's ability to undertake such a volume of work is explained by Walpole: 'His method of working, as a statuary, was to *bost*, as they call it, to hew out his heads from the block, and except some few finishing touches, to leave the rest to his workmen.'[15] Taylor's finest monumental work is probably the statue in Grendon Church, Warwick, of Miss Mary Chetwynd, who died in 1750, aged ninety-one; shortly after came his prize commission, that for the monument to General Guest (1660–1747) in Westminster Abbey which is dated 1752.

After the Guest monument, Walpole states, 'Taylor relinquished statuary unless incidentally a house ornament, and confined his pursuits to architecture'.[16] The change, however, was probably more gradual than Walpole implies: there are a series of church monuments by Taylor of 1752–5 and one at Pinner in Middlesex to Edmund Auberry of 1767. And in a document of 1758 relating to his house in Spring Gardens he is described as 'Robert Taylor, Statuary'.[17]

Taylor's first datable architectural work was carried out at the house of Peter Du Cane (1713–1803) in St James's Square in 1748–50 at an estimated cost of some £1,100. Payments included £267 for a statuary marble chimney-piece and £413 for alterations and furniture. Taylor carried out further work for Du Cane at Braxted Lodge in Essex which Du Cane had acquired in July 1751. On 2 September 1752 Taylor was paid for a journey he made there the previous year. Payments to Taylor continued over the next five years, concluding on 20 March 1756 with £21 4s 0d for 'repairs and rebuilding a part of Braxted Lodge'.[18] Later alterations make identification of Taylor's work difficult but the house retains some of his characteristic octagonal glazing and the entrance hall has another Taylor hallmark, a screen of columns at either end. Taylor was also paid for a chimney-piece.

By the mid-1750s, however, Taylor's architectural practice

was well under way. There are payments for Harleyford in 1755, indications of work at Barlaston in 1756, while 35 and 36 Lincoln's Inn Fields were occupied in 1757.

Some vivid details of Taylor's life and working habits are provided by Walpole: 'What the king of Prussia did for Science, Taylor did for trade; he never slept after four in the morning. When he had any journey, he did it in the night, and thus never but in a carriage, slept at all. When other people were at diversions he was in bed. His diet, medically prescribed him, was little animal food, and no wine.'[19] At the end of his life this harsh regime mellowed just a little. 'His common beverage', Walpole wrote, 'was water, and it was not till very lately, that after fruit, of which he was very fond, he indulged in a single glass of white wine; his evenings were wholly devoted to a beloved and affectionate wife, and a select company of sensible friends.'[20]

Taylor amassed a vast fortune that amounted to £180,000 at his death – a figure worth comparing with the £700,000 left by Sir Gilbert Heathcote, one of the founders of the Bank of England and reputedly the richest commoner in the country, at his death in 1733. 'There is no instance in art like it,' Walpole wrote. 'Kent died worth 10,000*l*. Gibbs had about 25,000*l*. Sir C. Wren had 50,000*l*.'[21] Given Taylor's impecunious beginnings it is remarkable that by 1768 (according to the *London Chronicle*) he was already worth £40,000 and his professional income was £8,000 a year at a time when he was spending just £800 a year.[22]

Taylor's fortune, accrued initially from professional fees, was greatly increased by shrewd investments. The *London Chronicle* continued:

In his ideas of property, he was like Lord Hardwicke and Lord Mansfield he averted from the funds. Except the necessary sum to qualify for a vote in Bank stock, he had no money invested in public securities. Irish mortages were the favorite employment of his money. He had 70,000*L* on one mortgage; 36,000*L* on another, 15,000*L* on a third. And when he offered 48,000*L* for an estate in Buckinghamshire for his son 'it was understood that he meant not to disturb any former investment'.

Taylor was also very fortunate in his purchase of the two houses at Spring Gardens where he built his own house. He acquired these 'of two brothers, for an annuity, and they both died in a year and a half'.

Taylor's financial success is the more impressive as he never received any major public commissions – the Bank of England at this time was independent of government. A considerable part of his earnings undoubtedly came from his activities as a surveyor. Walpole refers to 'surveyorship and agencies out of number'.[23] These included the Pulteney, Bath and Grafton estates in London. His appointment as Surveyor to the Bank of England dates from 1764 and here, he was active in purchasing property as well as extending the Bank's premises. He was also, according to Walpole, Surveyor to the Admiralty as well as to the Foundling Hospital and Lincoln's Inn.

In March 1769 Taylor joined the Office of Works as one of the two Architects of the Works; in 1777 he was appointed Master Carpenter and in 1780 became Master Mason and Deputy Surveyor.[24] Both these posts, however, were abolished in 1782 in Burke's reforms attacking sinecures. Payments show that Taylor was involved in overseeing the works at King's Bench and Fleet prisons, though Kenton Course seems to have been the architect in charge.[25] *The World* for 13 August 1787 also mentions his name in connection with Cold Baths Field prison in Middlesex: 'The Architecture, both as to general effect of the whole building, and the practical detail of each particular part, need not be doubted. There is James Payne and Sir Robert Taylor to see that all is right.'[26]

The Minutes of the Office of Works for these years show that Taylor was exceptionally conscientious in attending the regular weekly meetings throughout the year, for example missing just two meetings in 1770, two in 1771, none in 1772 and one in 1773.[25] This shows that his absences from London must have been short, and confirms Walpole's observation that he always travelled at night to save time. Taylor was also active in public life as a magistrate first at Westminster and then in the City, and in 1783 he was knighted on his election as Sheriff of London.[27]

Taylor is often said to have established the pattern of the modern architectural profession. While many eighteenth-century architects, notably the Adams at the Adelphi, were involved in large-scale speculative building, Taylor, according to the *London Chronicle*, 'was *never interested in the profit of any work* – but confined his emolument merely to the customary commission'. At the Bank of England this was 5 per cent on building works and 2½ per cent on property acquisition.

Taylor was one of the first architects to take pupils in the modern sense, as opposed to apprentices. Among these were Charles Beazley, T. Burnell, George Byfield, S. P. Cockerell, C. A. Craig, John Leach (who turned to law), John Nash and William Pilkington. According to Walpole, Taylor 'ever made it a point through life, to protect, support and recommend' his most capable pupils and even on his death bed 'suspended the consolations of religion, literally full half an hour, till he had finished various letters in favour of Mr Cockerell and Mr Craig the architects, to get them new patronage to secure them better in what they had got! In half an hour after he died.'[28]

Taylor was buried in great pomp in a vault in St Martin-in-the-Fields. Walpole[29] describes the solemn scene as a candlelit procession made its way from Spring Gardens to the church beginning with 'Two mutes, dressed in black' magistrates of Middlesex, two and two forty charity girls, in deep mourning, maintained at the expense of the parish two and two, followed by two parish beadles, church wardens and gentlemen of the vestry, two and two, two mutes, eight clergy, the chaplain, then the body supported by six of Taylor's pupils followed by friends wearing black silk scarfs and hat bands.

The Times, however, then in its infancy, took a different view and in two successive issues poured scorn and venom on Taylor's funeral.[30]

Such was the late Sir Robert Taylor's vanity that he bequeathed one guinea to each little boy and girl that sung at the funeral, and scarfs and hatbands to all the justices that honoured his corpse with their presence ... The outward trappings of useless expense on this funeral drew together a vast concourse of people last night, and the crowd of vagabonds and pickpockets about nine and ten o'clock was so great at St Martin's church that many lost their watches, purses, handkerchiefs, cloaks etc.

2 Patronage

The pattern of Taylor's patronage is of exceptional interest. The overwhelming majority of his commissions came not from the landed gentry and the older nobility but from new men or from families whose wealth dated back only one or two generations. Most of his patrons were City men or had strong links with the City of London, and in some cases Taylor built them not only London houses or offices but suburban villas or country houses as well. These links also provide important supporting evidence in making stylistic attributions to Taylor which help compensate for lack of documentation. These patrons moved in a series of overlapping circles: they were bankers and directors of the Bank of England (where Taylor became Surveyor in 1764). They include several directors of the East India Company. Quite a number had estates and interests in the West Indies; another group was formed of government financiers and army contractors. With these go a series of soldiers and sailors of fortune. Finally there is a clutch of lawyers — two of whom lived in Lincoln's Inn Fields next to Lincoln's Inn, where Taylor was surveyor.

Many of them were Members of Parliament, but though active in pursuing their business interests in the House and changing their allegiances accordingly they rarely spoke, and an election squib in 1790 at Sir Gerard Vanneck, builder of Heveningham in 1790, might stand for them all: 'For twenty long years I have been independent, in the Senate a silent and constant attendant.'[1]

In tracing these connections, the biographical entries in the *History of Parliament* volumes on the House of Commons for 1715–54 and 1754–90 have been an invaluable source. In the 1750s and early 1760s many of these links revolve round the great political organiser of the day, the Duke of Newcastle (1693–1768). This is at once intriguing, for in *The Builder* of

1846[2] alterations to Newcastle's seat at Clumber in Nottinghamshire are ascribed to Taylor but the attribution has been discounted for lack of documentary evidence. However, in a Royal Academy lecture of 1845,[3] C. R. Cockerell (whose father was a pupil of Taylor) mentions a room at Clumber by Taylor with screens of columns at either end like the Court Room at the Bank of England. Subsequent alterations by Barry and demolition in 1938 have left no record of Taylor's work but Cockerell's independent corroboration puts Clumber back into Taylor's *œuvre*.

The other major political figure in Taylor's career was the 3rd Duke of Grafton (1735–1811). Taylor was the Duke's surveyor and built Grafton House in Piccadilly about 1760 and a series of fourteen handsome town houses on the Duke's estate in Grafton Street, Piccadilly. Grafton is best remembered by Walpole's scornful remark that he thought 'the world should be postponed to a whore and a horse race'. But his political rise had been spectacular and he deserves credit as a consistent advocate of conciliation with the American colonies. He had succeeded as Duke in 1757, and a few years later he emerged actively in the political arena, vigorously opposing Lord Bute's new Ministry. Between 1767 and 1770 he had been Prime Minister, and after his resignation took office as Lord Privy Seal under Lord North, only finally withdrawing over the American issue in 1775.

Several of the residents of the Grafton Street houses were members of Wildman's Club[4] – a dining society in Albemarle Street which came into existence in the winter of 1763–4 as the focal point of organised and aggressive opposition, and was one of the first such clubs to have a complete set of newspapers, pamphlets and broadsheets. One member was Lord Villiers (1735–1805),[5] a close political associate of Grafton and one of the founders of the club for whom 4 Grafton Street was completed in 1775. Lord Villiers was the second son of the 3rd Earl of Jersey and had succeeded his father as 4th Earl in 1769. He had followed his uncle, the Hon. Thomas Villiers (1709–86),[6] as MP for Tamworth. This provides another Taylor link as Taylor had carried out alterations to Villiers's seat at The Grove, Watford, probably about 1756. Other members of Wildman's Club living in Grafton Street were Arnold Nesbitt, who in 1772 moved into

5 Grafton Street, and Sir George Warren MP (1735–1801)[7] who lived at 1 Grafton Street.

Taylor's city links can be traced back to his return from Italy and perhaps even to his apprenticeship with Cheere, as Cheere had been commissioned to provide a statue of William III for the Bank of England in 1731. After his father's death he had found immediate support from the Godfrey family of Woodford'[8] and 'his never failing friends' who were 'very respectable merchants in London' with a villa at Woodford of 'very ancient appearance opposite the church'.[9] The column Taylor created in gratitude to the family in 1771 still stands in the churchyard.[10]

Michael Godfrey (1659–95) was one of the first promoters of the Bank of England, being elected Deputy Governor in 1695. The same year his brother Peter Godfrey MP (1665–1724)[11] became a director of the Bank and also served as director of the East India Company between 1710 and 1718. His son Peter Godfrey (1695–1769), Taylor's principal friend, was a director of the East India Company for many years. A David Godfrey, probably his adopted son and heir, moved into Taylor's house at 35 Lincoln's Inn Fields from 1775 to 1778.[12]

Taylor may also have had early support from the Heathcote family, who had strong Bank of England connections. John Heathcote MP (*c.* 1689–1759)[13] was a director of the Bank of England (1725–35), a director of the East India Company (1716–24 and 1728–31) and President of the Foundling Hospital, where Taylor was one of the artists who in 1746 'agreed to present performances in their different professions for ornamenting the Hospital'.[14] In the *Architectural Publications Society's Dictionary* (1852–92) the Heathcote seat in Rutland, Normanton Hall, is ascribed to Taylor. There is no documentary evidence to support this but it may be that this is a confusion with work carried out elsewhere for the Heathcotes.

Taylor's first commission, according to Walpole, was a house for John Gore MP (*c.* 1689–1763)[15] of Bush Hill, Edmonton, at 112 Bishopsgate Street. Gore's father, Sir William, had been a director of the Bank of England and Gore himself was a Hamburg merchant and one of the original directors of the South Sea Company. He was included in the Disqualifying Act of 1720 after the collapse of the company but 'being a man of very fair character, he obtained an act, reversing his attainder'[16] and was allowed to retain £20,000 out of a fortune valued at nearly £39,000. He subsequently became a leading government contractor, obtaining contracts for remittances for British troops abroad and for subsidies to foreign governments totalling over £5 million between 1741 and 1752, on which he received commissions of between 5 and 15 per cent. Newcastle consulted him regularly on Treasury affairs.

Among bankers Taylor's principal patrons were Sir Charles Asgill (*d.* 1788)[17] and Sir George Colebrooke. For Asgill he designed a banking house at 70 Lombard Street (*c.* 1756), Asgill House at Richmond (1764) and the present Lord Mayor's Coach – made for Asgill's term in office as Mayor in 1757. Between 1768 and 1773 Asgill also occupied No. 14 St James's Square (on the site of the London Library) where Taylor had carried out works for Peter Du Cane.[18] Asgill had begun life as an outdoor collecting clerk at the Lombard Street Bank and 'from this inferior situation', his obituary in the *Gentleman's Magazine* relates, 'he progressively rose by his merit to the first department in the house; and soon after marrying an amiable woman with a fortune of 25,000*l* immediately joined his name to the firm'. At his death he was said to be worth £160,000 – only a little less than Taylor himself.

For Sir George Colebrooke (1729–1809)[19] Taylor carried out alterations at his villa at Arnos Grove, Southgate, about 1765. In addition he designed a domed mausoleum at Chilham Church in Kent for his brother Robert Colebrooke MP (1718–84).[20] Sir George was a banker and director of the East India Company between 1767 and 1773, twice serving as chairman. According to Mrs Thrale's *Diary* he inherited £130,000, and his wife (a Miss Gayner of Antigua) brought him a further £50,000:[21]

This wealth however could not content his imagination, which was ever busy among Schemes of further profit and further pleasure. From an elegant house at Southgate he removed to a splendid and expensive seat at Gatton in Surrey, from Broad Street in the City he hastened to Arlington Street St James's, where he occupied the Duke of Leinster's magnificent Habitation with more magnificence than his noble predecessor.

In the 1770s, however, Colebrooke overstretched himself by speculating in raw materials (losing £190,000 in a single speculation on hemp) and in a futile attempt to establish a world corner in alum. In 1773 his bank closed its doors and in 1777 a commission of bankruptcy was taken out against him.

Among Colebrooke's associates one, who evidently shared his taste for grand living was Arnold Nesbitt MP (1721–79).[22] Nesbitt moved into 5 Grafton Street in 1775 and was Mrs Thrale's brother-in-law. 'That Nesbitt', she wrote in 1791, 'was a shockingly wicked fellow.'[23] The Nesbitts were a landed family from Lismore in Ireland but Arnold Nesbitt had been apprenticed to his uncle Albert (d. 1753), a London merchant, and became his partner and heir. Nesbitt and Colebrooke were concerned together in a Dublin bank. In 1763 Lord Shelburne reported 'an underhand scheme' involving them both in the purchase of stock in Dominica, while in 1787 Nesbitt's nephew, John Nesbitt MP (? 1745–1817),[24] of Keston Park, Kent, also appears as a resident in a new house at 20 Grafton Street. John Nesbitt had been a partner in the Dublin bank. Mr Fordyce,[25] another Grafton Street resident, was a banker until his bankruptcy in 1781. Mrs Thrale says 'Fordyce began the world an adventurer' and amassed – by 'the *Gaming* method of commerce called *speculation* – more than three hundred thousand pounds'.

Another banking connection is provided by Peter Du Cane (1713–1803),[26] for whom Taylor worked in St James's Square and at Braxted Lodge, Essex. Du Cane was a director of the Bank of England (1755–83) and a director of the East India Company (1750–73). His father Richard (d. 1744) had also been a Bank of England director. A city link may have brought Taylor his only known commission in Cornwall – for alterations at Trewithen in 1763–4 which include one of his characteristic dining rooms with an arcade at either end. These were carried out for Thomas Hawkins MP (? 1724–66)[27] who had married Anne, the daughter of James Heywood of Austin Friars, in 1756.

Colebrooke and Du Cane have all been mentioned as East India Company directors. Another was Robert Thornton MP (1759–1826)[28] of Clapham, Surrey, a director between 1787 and 1814 who appears to have been the first established resident at 6 Grafton Street. Henry Crabb Boulton MP (c. 1709–73),[29] for whom Taylor built Thorncroft, at Leatherhead in 1772, was also a director of the East India Company as his father Richard had been from 1753 until his death. He was also involved with Colebrooke in speculative dealing in East India stock in 1771. Seven years earlier Clive had described him as a great rogue. Nesbitt's successor at 5 Grafton Street from 1780 to 1785, Sir Robert Smyth, Bt, MP (1744–1802)[30], also spoke out forcefully against Fox's East India Bill, describing the proposed abolition of the Court of Directors as 'presposterous' in 1783.

Nesbitt and Colebrooke's West India connections have already been mentioned. Another strong West Indies link comes with Sir John Boyd Bt (1718–1800)[31] for whom Taylor built Danson Park at Bexleyheath, 33 Upper Brook Street, and 7 Grafton Street. Boyd had inherited West India property through his mother, daughter of Judge Peters, on the Island of St Kitts. Boyd, who was also an East India Company director, appears at 7 Grafton Street (now the Medici Gallery) in 1774, being followed by his son, also John Boyd, in 1784. At No. 8 Grafton Street was Sir Ralph Payne MP (1739–1807),[32] who was created Baron Lavington in 1795. His father, also Ralph, had been Chief Justice of St Kitts and he himself was Governor of the Leeward Islands almost continuously from 1771 to his death. He obtained his seat in Parliament following a recommendation from a cousin to the Duke of Grafton. In politics he was an ally of Fox, and his Grafton Street house became a favourite resort of the Opposition leaders. Payne was renowned for his lavish entertaining: Erskine, when taken ill after an evening in 8 Grafton Street, sent a delightful riposte to Lady Payne's anxious inquiries about his condition: *'Tis true I am ill, but I need not complain; For he never knew pleasure who never knew Payne.'*

At 9 Grafton Street lived Sir John Taylor Bt (1745–86),[33] who had extensive estates in Jamaica. Details of his life have been kindly supplied by a descendant, Mrs Diana Phillips. He had been sent to school in England and had later gone on the Grand Tour, and acquired a taste for collecting. 'He then set up in London as a connoisseur and man of fashion to the annoyance of his elder brother Simon who was supporting him and his debts by sugar-planting in Jamaica.' On 17 December 1778 he married Elizabeth, daughter of Philip Houghton the younger of Hanover in Jamaica. As a result John came into various plantations in Hanover and was compelled to return there following a series of disastrous hurricanes and general lack of economy.

The West Indian links do not end in Grafton Street. John Freeman (d. 1794)[34] for whom Taylor had built Chute Lodge in Wiltshire (*c.* 1765), was the younger son of John Cooke (d. 1752), an East India merchant, who had taken the name of Freeman on succeeding to the estates of his uncle, William Freeman of St Kitts and Fawley. John's father had married Susanna Sambrooke, while John Gore (*c.* 1689–1753), for whom Taylor built a house in Bishopsgate, married Hanna Sambrooke. The two girls were sisters, and daughters of Sir Jeremy Sambrooke of North Mymms and Bush Hill. And Bishop Shute Barrington (1734–1826),[35] for whom Taylor had done gothic work at the Bishop's Palace at Salisbury soon after 1782, was brother of Samuel Barrington (1729–1800), admiral and commander-in-chief in the West Indies in 1778. There may even be a West Indies link here with Longford Castle, near Salisbury, where Taylor was paid for work in 1751 and 1761 for the 1st Viscount Folkestone. His son, the Hon. William Bouverie (1725–1776),[36] who succeeded in 1761, had married in 1751 Rebecca, daughter of John Alleyne of Barbados. In turn his son, Jacob Pleydell-Bouverie (1750–1828),[37] paid for the Guildhall at Salisbury, built to Taylor's designs after Taylor's death in 1788. Among the Bouverie papers in the Northamptonshire Record Office is a design for a farm building signed and dated 'Robert Taylor 1769'.

Another overlapping group is formed by those of Taylor's patrons who were active either as government financiers or in handling contracts for victuals and wages to troops abroad. These were indeed rich prizes: Sir Lewis Namier considered that 'even the fattest sinecure could not equal the profits to be had from contracts'.[38] Not surprisingly, Newcastle was at the centre of many of the dealings with Taylor's patrons. On 12 December 1759 he wrote to Bath: 'The sum to be raised this year ... was so great, that I found it absolutely necessary to agree it with the principal and most responsible men in the City.'[39] Of the £2,986,000 raised, £466,000 came from the Bank of England, £330,000 from the South Sea Company (via John Gore),

£200,000 from Mr Godfrey at the East India Company, £1,200,000 from Sir Joshua Vanneck & Co. (whose son Sir Gerard was to commission Heveningham), £480,000 from James Colebrooke (elder brother of Sir George), and £350,000 from Mr Nesbitt. That Taylor's patrons, or their families and relations, could raise such substantial loans is an amazing indication of their resources.

During the Seven Years War Nesbitt held a series of army contracts[40] for sending remittances to troops in America in 1756 and for victualling troops in Louisburg, Quebec and Guadaloupe in 1759–60. He continued to hold them after peace in 1763, with a victualling contract for 6,000 men in North America in 1783.

Another major army contractor was Peter Taylor MP (1714–77)[41] for whom Taylor built Purbrook House, near Portsmouth. Taylor, who was no relation of Sir Robert (or Sir John), was born in Wells, the son of a grocer. 'It was my misfortune', he wrote, 'to lose my parents at the age of thirteen. I was turned into the wide world without a friend, without learning, with a small fortune to begin with.' At the outbreak of the Seven Years War in 1756 he was appointed a deputy paymaster in Germany. At the height of the fighting £150,000 was passing through his hands and Newcastle in 1760 wrote to General Mostyn puzzling over 'the payments in light dollars instead of heavy ones'. Soon ugly rumours were circulating and when James Harris met Peter Taylor at a dinner party of Lord Shelburne's in 1763 he could not rid himself of the idea of '£400,000 got in four years'. Among the friends at Taylor's funeral was William Devaynes MP (*c.* 1730–1809)[42] of Dover Street and Pall Mall, who was handling victualling contracts for 12,000–14,000 men in America during the War of Independence. He was also a director of the East India Company from 1770 to 1805.

A number of Taylor's patrons were receiving secret-service pensions. Robert Colebrooke held a secret-service pension of £600 between 1756 and 1761;[43] Sir Thomas Sewell received secret-service disbursements towards the costs of his unsuccessful election campaign at Wallingford in 1754.[44]

Sir Thomas Sewell MP (1710–1784)[45] had in 1757 moved into 35 Lincoln's Inn Fields, one of a pair of houses built to Taylor's designs in 1754–6. He also had a country villa by Taylor,

Ottershaw Park near Chertsey, begun soon after 1761. According to his obituary in the *Gentleman's Magazine* he had been bred up under an attorney and 'afterwards engaged in the laborious business of a draughtsman in Chancery'. By 1764, when he was knighted, he was supposed to be making £3,000–£4,000 a year. He was a protégé of Newcastle and when he failed to win a seat at Wallingford in 1754 Newcastle obtained Harwich for him four years later. In 1764 he was appointed Master of the Rolls, which reputedly surprised no one more than Sewell himself.

His neighbour in 36 Lincoln's Inn Fields, who is also first entered in the rate books in 1757, was Sir (Anthony) Thomas Abdy MP, Bt (?1720–75)[46] of Chobham Place, Surrey, and Albyns in Essex. Abdy's practice according to the *History of Parliament* 'was in Chambers rather than at the bar, and more akin to an attorney's than a barrister's; he specialized in family business and in cases concerning landed property'.

It would be fascinating to know if there was any link between Sewell and Abdy and Thomas Mills (1717–1804),[47] an attorney of Leek in Staffordshire for whom Barlaston was built in 1756–7. This the very same moment the two houses in Lincoln's Inn Fields were rising and No. 35 and Barlaston have many features in common. Mills was a country attorney who had made a good match: he had married in 1742 Esther co-heiress of Samuel Bagnall (d. 1741). At the time of their marriage, she was described as 'a young lady of between £6,000 and £7,000 in fortune'. She had become sole owner of the Barlaston estate which the Bagnalls had acquired in 1671.

Thomas Mills's father, William (1689–1749), is described as 'an eminent attorney of Leek' in *Aris's Birmingham Gazette*. Another William Mills (d. 1695), presumably his grandfather, was also an attorney. Both Thomas and his father evidently also had quite substantial houses in Leek. John Sleigh in his *History of Leek* (1862) quotes a letter saying that at the time of the 1745 Rebellion, when the rebels came to Leek 'Their Princes lay at old Mr Mills ... Ld Elco at Young Mills'.

The next group of Taylors patrons were sailors and soldiers. One of these, Captain Philemon Pownoll,[48] had the great good fortune to capture in 1762, without resistance, the richest prize of the Seven Years War – the *Hermione* – a Spanish Register ship from Lima. Captain Pownoll's share was £64,872 13s 9d. With this he bought the Sharpham Estate in 1765 and largely rebuilt the existing house to Taylor's designs about 1770.

It would be interesting to know whether Pownoll had been pointed to Taylor by another sailor, Lord Howe (1726–99),[49] the great naval commander known to his sailors as Black Dick on account of his swarthy appearance. Certainly the two men knew each other – for in 1778 Pownoll sailed as Captain of the *Apollo* in Lord Howe's fleet. For Howe, Taylor built 3 Grafton Street and soon after 1772 Porter's Lodge in Hertfordshire. Howe was also a Lord of the Admiralty in 1763–65 and may have been responsible for Taylor's appointment as Surveyor to the Admiralty. He also had West Indies links – his father had been Governor of Barbados (a post said to be worth £7,000 a year) when he died in 1735. The building lease, shows that Howe's house was actually built by the Hon. John Bourgoyne MP (1723–99)[50] better known as General Bourgoyne. Bourgoyne was another of Grafton's supporters and in 1772, encouraged, it is thought, by Grafton, he proposed that a House of Commons Select Committee should be established to examine the East India Company – and became its Chairman. Bourgoyne, like Admiral Howe and his brother General Howe, was a leading figure in the fighting in North America – it is perhaps not entirely coincidence that Nesbitt, Howe's neighbour in Grafton Street, should have been one of the principal army victualling contractors.

General Bourgoyne's involvement in building 3 Grafton Street helps support the attribution of a very handsome room at The Oaks, Carshalton (now demolished, and not to be confused with the room designed by Adam in the same house), for Lord Derby. According to Prosser's *Select Illustrations of Surrey* (1828) The Oaks was originally a small house built by 'a society of gentlemen called The Hunter's Club. . . . General Bourgoyne purchased the lease of the club, and added to and improved the house. . . . On the ground floor is a good dining room, built by General Bourgoyne, forty-two feet in length by twenty-one in breadth, including an arched recess at each end, and eighteen feet in height. It is ornamented with twenty-six small cased corinthian columns, bearing a cornice; various medallions also adorn the walls'. This room has close parallels with the ground-floor room at 4 Grafton Street while the short columns echo C. R. Cockerell's comments on the Court Room at the Bank of England: 'the order is very small,' he said in one of his Royal Academy lectures.[51]

Another interesting link is provided by Lord Howe's sister, the Hon. Mrs Caroline Howe,[52] who lived at 12 Grafton Street from 1771 until her death in 1807. Wraxall in his *Memoirs* notes that she was a granddaughter of George I and 'continued to wear the female costume of that reign at the close of the 18th century and her figure cast in a Westphalian mould, baffled all description'. Benjamin Franklin who became a friend of Mrs Howe describes his meeting with Lord Howe at her house on 'Christmas Day evening', 1774. Lord Howe expressed concern at the situation in America and asked Franklin to draw up proposals which might lead to a reconciliation. Though they had several subsequent meetings at No. 12 nothing came of their proposals and Lord Howe of course became Admiral of the Fleet off the American coast. It is interesting nonetheless that Howe, like the Duke of Grafton, was an advocate of conciliation with the American colonies.

Mrs Howe was a great friend of Countess Spencer and when the roof fell in Althorp in 1772 she managed the repairs during Lord and Lady Spencer's absence abroad. Correspondence at Althorp[53] shows that Taylor supervised these repairs and the same year Taylor was also working at Spencer House in London. Mrs Howe wrote: 'Pray say what Lord Spencer determined as to the London staircase. I shall probably not see Taylor a great while was he with you before you went?'

From all these links between different patrons it is very clear how Taylor's vast practice was built up very much on personal recommendations. From the handful of works mentioned by Walpole and the buildings illustrated by Malton, the list of Taylor's works begins to justify Hardwick's comment that Taylor and James Paine 'nearly divided the practice of the profession between them till Mr Robert Adam entered the lists'.[54]

3 Villas

Taylor's major contribution to English architecture is his ingenious and original development of the Palladian villa. The first generation of Palladian villas in Britain – Chiswick, Mereworth and Stourhead are three leading examples – had all been based purposely very closely on Palladio's designs. They were square or rectangular in plan with pedimented porticoes, and a 1–3–1 arrangement of windows on the principal elevations. Taylor broke with this format. First of all all his villas (like his town houses) were astylar: classical in proportion but without an order, that is without columns or pilasters and with a simple cornice instead of a full entablature.

Secondly, most of Taylor's villas were set apart in the landscape, often in exposed positions, with commanding views to and from the house. This was the exact antithesis of the traditional site of a country house which Walpole described aptly at Euston: 'It stands as all old houses do, for convenience of water and shelter, in a hole, so it neither sees nor is seen.'[1]

While most of Palladio's villas, however compact, tended to be aggrandised by colonnades and wings, Taylor's villas are usually isolated in the landscape like garden temples – an idealised vision of the country house in which farm buildings, stables and walled gardens are all banished from the immediate surroundings of the house.

Thirdly, Taylor's planning breaks radically from Palladian prototypes. Chiswick and Mereworth are on a noughts-and-crosses grid around a central domed hall or saloon, with small spiral staircases in the corners, following Palladio's view that staircases should be small and not upset the symmetry of the plan. Taylor by contrast placed his staircases in the centre of the house where no direct light was available except from above, with all the main rooms opening onto the staircase or entrance hall, so there was no need to go through one room to reach another.

Most of Taylor's villas have only four rooms on the principal floor – hall, saloon, dining room and library. The anterooms and cabinets that formed sets of apartments for husband, wife and guests in early eighteenth-century houses disappear. The bedrooms are almost always all above the main floor, anticipating modern modes of living.

How does a villa differ from a country house? Charles Middleton, writing in 1793, offered the following definition:

Villas may be considered under three different descriptions: first, as the occasional and temporary retreats of the nobility and persons of fortune from their town residence and must of course be in the vicinity of the metropolis; secondly, as country houses of wealthy citizens and persons in official stations which also cannot be far removed from the capital ... thirdly, the smaller kind of provincial edifices considered either as hunting seats or the habitations of country gentlemen of moderate fortune. Elegance, compactness and convenience are the characteristics of such buildings in contradistinction to the magnificent and extensive range of the country seats of our nobility and opulent gentry.[2]

Most of Taylor's villas as we have seen fell in the first or second group; they were built principally for city men or men who had made their own fortunes or had recently acquired them.

Chronologically the first group is formed by Harleyford, Coptfold and Barlaston, all dating from the 1750s and bearing strong rococo elements. The first by a short head appears to be Harleyford, which Langley's *History of the Hundred of Desborough* (1797)[3] says was built to Taylor's designs in 1755. It was commissioned for Sir William Clayton (*c.* 1718–83)[4], the second son of Sir William Clayton (d. 1744) of Marden Park, Surrey, the first Baronet, who had bought Harleyford in 1735. The elder Sir William in turn was nephew and heir of Sir Robert Clayton MP (1629–1707), who Evelyn described as 'a prodigious rich scrivener' or moneylender. As younger brother of Sir Kenrick, also an MP, William Clayton inherited the second seat.

A single set of payments in an estate account book in September 1755 confirms that the building was under way in 1755, with £356 3s paid on account for 'building Harleyford House' and £172 9s 8½d for moving ground.[5]

Patterson's Roads (1829) describes the house as a very convenient mansion 'sheltered by a fine grove from the cold blasts of the north', and there is a painting at Squerryes in Kent[6] showing it soon after it was built (Plate 25). The setting with the waterfall on the river is romanticised but the house is accurately depicted. The painting is important as it shows the canted bay at the side before it was raised to its present height. The plan of Harleyford is unusual as unlike all the later villas it has a canted bay on only one side – an asymmetrical, even rococo, touch (Plate 27). The house is of brick with stone dressings. Taylorian signatures are the octagonal glazing which survives in some of the windows and the vermiculated rustication around the basement windows (Plate 26). Over the canted bay was a Diocletian window similar to that at 35 Lincoln's Inn Fields. The entrance front has the triple arch which Taylor used on a number of occasions, for example at Chute and at 33 Upper Brook Street. Here the stonework appears renewed and changed in detail.

The house consists of a basement, a low ground floor, a *piano nobile* above, a half storey with the main bedrooms, and an attic storey concealed behind the parapet. Mrs Lybbe Powis, who visited Harleyford on 28 July 1767, noted that 'the whole of the offices are so contained in a pit as to be perfectly invisible – a great addition to the look of any place'.[7] This pit, old photographs suggest, was to some extent a ditch with an artificial terrace.

Immediately inside the front door Taylor makes great play with niches, vaults and domes – a cross-vaulted outer hall with niches on three bays, a domed and apsed inner hall or vestibule (very close to that at 35 Lincoln's Inn Fields) and a triple-domed corridor flanked with niches opening off to the right.[8] There are two staircases in the central core (Plate 27). The main staircase is of wooden construction with a Chinese Chippendale balustrade, and ascends in straight flights around an open well to an arcaded landing on the next floor (Plate 31). What is puzzling is the way the secondary or service stair emerges directly on to the landing by means of a curious trapdoor arrangement. As this feature recurs at several other villas it must nonetheless be original.

Harleyford has been empty and decaying for a considerable number of years, apart from the basement which has been used as a clubhouse in association with the caravan park in the grounds. However, the house was illustrated in *Country Life* in 1910,[9] when it still belonged to the Claytons, and the library and drawing room recorded when they were still furnished. The library is inset with blind arches containing bookcases (Plate 30) and circular recesses over the doorcases with busts – an architectural treatment repeated at Barlaston (Plate 36) and Chute. The doors have octagonal panels to match the glazing of the windows. The saloon has fine plasterwork trophies of hunting, shooting, fishing and boating – the treatment is naturalistic though there are rococo cartouches and S and C curves (Plate 29). The chimney-piece with the lion's head is similar to one at The Grove, Watford.

Taylor's next villa was Coptfold Hall, near Margaretting in Essex, demolished between 1848 and 1851.[10] This was built for Richard Holden who bought the estate, including the old manor, on 21 November 1755 and appears to have begun building at once. Both Madge's map of 1801 and Malton's view show that the house stood isolated, while a sale catalogue of 1828 states that it was 'delightfully seated on a considerable and very pleasing eminence, in a beautiful park of 166 acres' – intended again to see and be seen.

Once again the exterior is astylar, but this time there are canted bays on both sides, surmounted by Venetian windows (Plate 32). The front door and the openings on either side have octagonal panels – as at Harleyford – but the windows above are shown with plain sashes. The main floor is surmounted by one and a half storeys and Malton's view suggests that there was no basement. However, the 1828 sale catalogue speaks of an extensive and well lit one including a 'housekeeper's room, large servants' hall and knife room adjoining, a butler's pantry, a very capital kitchen and scullery and two larders'. Below this was a second level of vaulted cellars with a larder, dairy, scullery and wine cellars, while in front of the house, perhaps under the terrace shown by Malton, was 'a spacious area, with numerous extensive vaults' in which there was an ice-house – an interesting example of an ice-house apparently entered from the basement rather than an outside doorway in the grounds. The plan (Plate 33) is similar to that of Harleyford. The hall, or vestibule, as at Harleyford, is shallow with a central dome flanked by cross-vaults with pairs of columns in between. The staircase again rises around a square well and was probably of wood. To the right are two smaller cross-vaulted spaces (creating a sequence of three sizes of vaults diminishing telescopically) lead to a powdering room. This opens into the library, on the far side of which is a cabinet. These smaller rooms reflecting early eighteenth-century house plans which are eliminated in the later villas. On the opposite side the dining room has Taylor's characteristic arcades at either end. On the first floor the sale catalogue describes a handsome boudoir over the dining room, and four airy bedrooms with two dressing rooms, with a further four large airy bedrooms on the floor above.

Of Richard Holden virtually nothing is known but it is tempting to think he was related to Samuel Holden MP of Roehampton (*c.* 1675–1740),[11] who was a director of the Bank of England in 1720–7 and 1731–40 and a Governor of the Russia Company. His house, however, survived little more than a century and was presumably demolished about 1861–2 when, according to White's *Directory of Essex* (1863), a new house was erected about half a mile away.

The third villa in this group is Barlaston Hall. This was built for Thomas Mills (1717–1804), an attorney of Leek in the north of Staffordshire. Mills was sheriff of Staffordshire in 1754 and in 1742, a year after her father's death, had married Esther, daughter and co-heiress of Samuel Bagnall. She is described in *Aris's Birmingham Gazette* as 'a young lady of between £6,000 and £7,000 fortune'. Esther died in 1752 and not long after Thomas Mills began a new house on a new site. The date can be fixed from entries in the parish register first noted in a history of the village published in 1966.[12] In December 1756 this records the marriage of Thomas Sutton, a young bricklayer from Norwich, 'who had worked at his trade in the parish of Barlaston at the building of Mr Mills' house several months'.[13] The following November there is an entry for the baptism of a daughter of

Joseph Price, who is described as a stonecutter working for Mr Mills.[13] From this it is clear that Harleyford, Coptfold and Barlaston were all rising virtually simultaneously in 1755 and 1756.

Like the other two villas, Barlaston stands in a commanding position with a fine view westward over parkland sloping gently towards the river which has been widened at this point to look like a lake. William West's *Picturesque Views of Staffordshire and Shropshire* (1830) describes it as looking over 'the most delightful picturesque portion of the Vale of Trent ... backed and embosomed in trees'. Barlaston, he continues, not only 'commands the view of a vast tract of country, but can also, from its great elevation, be seen for many miles'. Once again Taylor chose a conspicuous position.

No documentation has been traced to show that Barlaston was designed by Taylor but there are so many parallels with Harleyford and Coptfold that the attribution seems beyond serious doubt. Only the weakness of certain details, such as the window architraves, suggest that Taylor may not have supervised the work very closely. The entrance front with one and a half storeys over the main floor is almost identical to Coptfold (Plate 34) – not only in proportion and arrangement but in details such as the string courses under the first-floor windows and the dentil cornice with a low parapet formed by coping stones. The balls on the pediment compare with those at Harleyford. The treatment of the front door-case is also similar to Coptfold, while the octagonal glazing is another Taylor signature. At the sides the treatment of the canted bays surmounted by Venetian windows enclosed in a relieving arch (Plate 35) is exactly as at Coptfold while the great elliptical bay on the garden front echoes that at both the other early villas.

The brick chosen was a dark red, at a distance a plum colour, and laid in Flemish bond with remarkably narrow lime mortar joints. For the elliptical bow specially shaped trapezoid bricks were used as headers to ensure a smooth curve. Unfortunately, early in the nineteenth century the house was rendered and though the plaster has since been removed the scoring of the bricks prior to rendering is still visible at close quarters.

Barlaston was empty and deteriorating for many years until in the autumn of 1981 it was acquired by Save Britain's Heritage. Yet as a result of this decay, of the removal of floorboards and the collapse of plasterwork, it has been possible to see the construction of the house in a way that is rare with eighteenth-century houses where so much is concealed behind interior finishes.

The plan has close parallels with both Harleyford and Coptfold (Plate 35). The ground falls away sharply to the west, so that, though the front door is only a short flight of steps above ground level at the sides and back the basement is in fact at ground level. Under parts of the house there is a sub-basement wholly below ground. To the north was the kitchen, where the floor was sunk to provide greater height. The rooms in the sub-basement were lit by small windows opening on to a concealed wall walk room running round the house (a feature found also at Danson and other villas) which served to air the lower rooms and keep the damp in the earth some distance away from the walls.

The hall at Barlaston has stone paving laid on the same octagon and diamond pattern as the windows. Beyond, the staircase, was again of wood (Plate 38). As at Harleyford it is of cantilever construction. The wooden treads were supported by zigzag wrought-iron bars which fitted beneath the risers and treads of each flight. The use of iron supports in this way enabled Taylor to cut away the underside of each step, giving it a scrolled profile and creating an effect of lightness such as earlier had only been possible with stone cantilevered staircases – for example Inigo Jones's Tulip Stair in the Queen's House at Greenwich. While many early eighteenth-century wooden staircases were finished underneath with scrolls, these scrolls were added beneath the box of the step, not cut into it.

The principal floor at Barlaston consists of the hall and three large main rooms, presumably library, drawing room and dining room as at Coptfold – without the cabinet or closet found there – showing Taylor moving towards the ideal treatment of his villas in the 1760s. The library (Plate 36) still retains some of the original octagonal and diamond pattern doors to the bookcases with matching octagonal panels on the shutters and in the window reveals. The blind arches in the walls and the recesses above an intermediate cornice are also very close to the library at

Harleyford. Opposite, in what was presumably the dining room, there are plaster trophies in the wall panels. At either end of the dining room are large panels for inset canvases, one of which contained a group portrait of Thomas Mills and his family, with a portrait head of his late wife floating ethereally in the background. The delicacy and lightness of the rococo surrounds to the frames suggests they might be a few years later than the much more vigorous and boldly modelled rococo overmantel above the fireplace. On the first floor Taylor placed one large bedroom over the drawing room but had to introduce smaller rooms over the other principal rooms. This meant cross-walls ending in the middle of the great Venetian windows over the canted bays, a solecism met with characteristic eighteenth-century nonchalance. The construction of these cross-walls, which could not weigh too heavily on the ceilings below, is of special interest: they are giant A-frames infilled with brick.

The next group of Taylor's villas all date from the 1760s – Danson Hill, near Bexleyheath in Kent (1762–7), Asgill House at Richmond (1761–4), and Chute Lodge in Wiltshire (*c.* 1768). With them probably goes a house of which much less is known, Ottershaw Park near Chertsey, Surrey, demolished in 1908 (Plate 48). An article in *The World* 7 (December 1787) on villas in Surrey and Middlesex states that the house was built for Thomas Sewell by Sir Robert Taylor.[14] According to Prosser's *Surrey* (1828), Sewell acquired the property in April 1761 and 'pulled down the old house and built the present mansion on higher ground' – a further instance of Taylor's preference for elevated sites. This was Sewell's second house by Taylor: he had moved into 35 Lincoln's Inn Fields in 1757. Prosser describes Ottershaw as 'a handsome and uniform brick structure raised on groined arches' – in other words a typical Taylor basement. Inside there was a library 'with a screen of columns at each end' and an elegant drawing-room, of octagonal form finished in the Chinese style, with circular dome ceiling.

Danson, Asgill and Chute show a subtle development on the villas of the 1750s. The earlier villas all had bold curved bows, semi-elliptical in shape, rising the full height of the garden front. In this group these are replaced by canted bays, with octagonal rather than D-shaped drawing rooms within. The earlier houses had roofs set back behind a low parapet: on the 1760s villas the roofs rest directly on a dentilled cornice.[15] Danson and Asgill were faced in ashlar, while Chute and Ottershaw like the earlier villas were entirely of brick.

Danson Hill is included among the engravings of Taylor's work published by Malton in 1790–2.[16] It was built for John Boyd for whom Taylor later built 33 Upper Brook Street and 7 Grafton Street. In 1753 Boyd had taken out a lease of the old manor house at Danson which had stood in the bottom of the valley to the south of the site of the new house. Six years later he purchased the freehold. He had to obtain a private Act of Parliament in 1762 to allow him to demolish certain properties to which charitable strings were attached. The Act expresses his intention to demolish the old house and to spend at least £2,500 on a new house and out-offices. Work was to be completed within five years and probably began immediately.

The new house was built in an elevated position (Plate 39) with commanding views over the park down to a large lake, but actually stands on a level site. The main floor is raised on a full rusticated basement (Plate 41), and the front door is approached by an unusually broad and imposing flight of steps leading not to the grand portico that might be expected but to an open terrace with a simple columned door-case. Beneath the terrace, at the sides, are arched entrances to the basement, treated with Taylor's characteristic vermiculated rustication. Later alterations detract somewhat from the crispness of Taylor's design: the original Bath stone facing has been covered with a cold white rendering and the window architraves have been crudely simplified. An extra storey has been added to the canted bays at the sides, obliterating the subtle contrast in height with the bay on the garden front, while two flat-roofed extensions have been built in the angles of the entrance front.

Danson, unlike Coptfold and Barlaston, has only a half storey over the main floor though, as at Harleyford, there are rooms in the attic. This adherence to Palladian models brought a cryptic comment from the *Kentish Traveller's Companion* in 1776 – that 'the diminutive size' of the upper windows suggested 'the architect did not imagine that sleeping in airy chambers might contribute to the health of the family who might inhabit this mansion.'

In saying this the author sensed the mood of the times for towards the end of the eighteenth century country houses again largely reverted to the seventeenth-century arrangement of two even or almost even ranks of windows on the ground and first floors.

Danson, it appears, was originally intended to stand isolated like the other early villas but Hasted mentions that while building was in progress it was decided to extend the building by a pair of detached wings linked to the house by quadrant walls. These are shown in Malton's view and though no trace of the wings survives today the *Ambulator* in 1782 mentions handsome wings and they are also shown in the 1799 Ordnance Survey. *Patterson's Roads* (1829) notes that the wings of the house were subsequently pulled down 'and a large pile of stabling and offices erected'. The grounds, he adds, 'were laid out by the celebrated Brown, who also formed a spacious sheet of water'. The change of plan may have been promoted by Boyd's second marriage in 1766 to Catherine, daughter of the Rev. John Chapone at Charlton, Gloucestershire.

Like the earlier villas, Danson has both a basement (here a ground floor) and a partial sub-basement lit from a dry walk running right round the house. The basement contains a large vaulted kitchen and other office quarters but three of the rooms here have original classical chimney-pieces, suggesting they may have been family rather than servants' rooms.

The main floor (Plate 40) is composed of four large rooms marked on Malton's plan as hall, dining room, saloon and library, with a central oval stone cantilevered stair. Between the basement and the main floor the treads and the iron railing are plain; above, the steps have the scrolled undersides found on many of Taylor's staircases and a more elaborate balustrade. The first-floor landing is ringed by an Ionic colonnade carrying an oval dome with an oculus lighting the stairwell. Here the balustrade is again different, this time of wood. Once again there is the curious arrangement of the secondary stair rising straight through the floor of the landing. Certain elements of the interior decoration were carried out by Chambers rather than Taylor but the ceiling of the octagonal room, identical to that at Chute Lodge, must be by Taylor while the library has the circular recesses in the upper walls found at Harleyford and Barlaston.

The next of these 1760s villas is Asgill House on the Thames at Richmond.[17] On 30 May 1761, Sir Charles Asgill, for whom Taylor had built a banking house at 70 Lombard Street (Plate 7), acquired for £735 from the executors of the late Moses Hart the lease of a narrow strip of land at the bottom of what is now Old Palace Lane. Taylor acted as his agent in this transaction. In June and July 1762 Asgill petitioned for a new lease in consideration of pulling down former buildings, erecting a substantial new house and rebuilding the coach house, stables and domestic offices. The Surveyor General's report of 12 August 1762 states that none of the buildings are yet finished and Asgill's name first appears in the rate book in 1764. A submission to the Crown in 1810 by a later occupant states that the house cost £6,000–£7,000.

At Asgill Taylor once again built on a prominent site where the new house could both see and be seen (Plate 45). The treatment of the river front is highly unusual for it is a variant of Palladio's pediment-within-a-pediment used at the Redentore at Venice and other churches, and adopted by William Kent for the temple at Euston. Taylor varies Palladio's motif in an unexpected way for the inner and upper pediment is only implied in the shape of the roof line – a reduction to essentials that shows Taylor advancing from Palladianism to neoclassicism. A parallel primitivist touch of which the Abbé Laugier, the great neoclassical protagonist, would surely have approved are the simple barn-like eaves, inspired probably by Inigo Jones's St Paul's Covent Garden (which Jones had of course described as the greatest barn in Christendom).

The villa has a high rusticated 'basement' which is in fact the main floor. This allows a full storey for the main bedrooms above with a half storey for the attic rooms in the centre, an arrangement of which the author of the *Kentish Traveller's Companion* would surely have approved. In plan Asgill is shallower than the other villas – there is no space for windows to either side of the canted bays on the flanks of the house (Plate 46). As a result there was no possibility of a central top-lit stair and Taylor instead contrived a hall and stair in matching ovals on either side of a central vaulted entrance hall. The staircase is a miniature *tour de force* (Plate 47). To save space it does not rise direct to the second floor but branches off on the first-floor landing and rises neatly under the sloping eaves, making use of an otherwise wasted space. This in turn led to the introduction of an elegant serpentine in the landing and a beautiful cross-vista through two Venetian arches – once again ingeniously compressed in dimensions because of shortage of space. In the attic storey Taylor contrived a pair of oval bedrooms in the octagonal core, here with straight sides and semicircular ends. This solved the problem of creating two rooms behind a canted bay though it did mean that the central window lights only a lobby.

Chute Lodge, north west of Andover but in Wiltshire was built for John Freeman, the younger son of an East Indian merchant, whose family had first made their money in the West Indies. He had married Elizabeth Strickland in 1751 and soon after they settled at Chute. There was an earlier house here – in Salisbury Cathedral there is a tomb of 1673 to Susanna Maria, daughter of 'Johnnis Collins de Chute Lodge'.[18]

Josiah Wedgwood in a letter of 7 September 1771 to Mr Bentley mentions a visit to Etruria by Mr Freeman of Schute Lodge, who, he says, 'has travelled and is a man of Taste ... *he admires our works exceedingly* ... he is a great admirer of Young Flaxman and has advised his Father to send him to Rome, which he has promised to do. Mr Freeman says he knows young Flaxman is a Coxcomb, but does not think him a bit the worse for it, or the less likely to be a great Artist.'[19] John Freeman may also have dabbled in architecture like his father, who was an amateur architect of some ability. There is an unexecuted design for the octagon room at Chute inscribed 'J Freeman's Room at Chute in 1768'.[20]

This is the nearest there is to a date for the house and corresponds with an advertisement in the *Salisbury and Winchester Journal* of 14 September 1795, announcing that Chute was for sale and stating that the house had been built 'within thirty years at the expense of 8,000*l* upwards'.[21] The attribution to Taylor was initially made on stylistic grounds, particularly some very close parallels with Danson, but confirmation comes in a manuscript note of 2 September 1882 entitled 'Early History of Chute Lodge' kindly supplied to me by Mr Michael Fowle, whose ancestors had acquired the house about 1805.[22]

This states: 'Chute Lodge was built by Mr Freeman. The architect he employed was Sir Robert Taylor, a man much esteemed at that period.' Though the note was written over a century later it seems unlikely that Taylor's name would have been attached to the house without good reason. The memoir continues: 'Mr Freeman had resided many years in Italy indeed so long that in some of his domestic arrangements he must have thought more of Italian skies and Italian sun than the ... uncertain climate of England. The house was partly copied from the Aldobrandini Borghese Palazzo.'

The roof of Chute has been altered but an early drawing shows the central pediment above the cornice line of the rest of the roof a little like the villa Aldobrandini at Frascati. This drawing confirms that the bracketed cornice, like that at Asgill, is original, or close to the original. It also shows the steps up to the terrace in front of the first floor entrance rose in semicircular flights. The triple arcade here is similar to Harleyford. The basement at Chute is rusticated as at Danson. On the garden side (Plate 42) the tall arched windows to the octagon have the vermiculated rustication of which Taylor was so fond, as do all the basement windows.

The 1795 sale announcement includes 900 acres of land round the house 'a large part of which is enclosed with pales, and ornamented with extensive plantations and rides in the best taste, by Brown and Emes'. The tithe map of 1840 shows that Chute like the other villas stood isolated from the offices – the stables and walled gardens were some hundreds of yards away.

Internally Chute also corresponds closely to Danson, notably the vaulted kitchen in the basement and the almost identical oval staircase (Plate 43) with a dome supported on a ring of Ionic columns. The octagon room (Plate 44) on the main floor has, as has already been mentioned, the same ceiling as the one at Danson while the library has the characteristic roundels.

Taylor's last two villas are Purbrook House on Portsdown Hill just north of Portsmouth (*c.* 1770) and Sharpham House, outside Totnes in Devon (*c.* 1770). Purbrook was built for Peter Taylor, who acquired the estate in 1764 with the fortune he had amassed as an army contractor in the Seven Years War. *White's Directory for Hampshire* (1878) gives a date of 1770 – probably that of completion.

Sadly, Purbrook House was demolished in 1829[23] and is known only in three plates by Malton, but it was undoubtedly one of Taylor's finest and most elaborate houses. Externally Taylor adopts the Palladian formula of corner towers familiar from Wilton and Holkham and used a smaller scale by Roger Morris in a number of villas in the 1730s and 1740s. Characteristically, Taylor's treatment is astylar (Plate 49), giving no hint of the grandeur within. This severity is once again neo-classical as much as Palladian. Malton shows Purbrook with four wings containing washhouse and laundry, kitchen and two sets of stables. These were linked to the house not by corridors as, say, at Kedleston but simply by low quadrant walls like those at Danson, a curious arrangement as far as food was concerned.

Malton's plan (Plate 50) shows that Purbrook was considerably larger than the earlier villas. On the principal floor are hall, saloon and drawing room, library and common parlour, and dressing room. There is, however, no principal bedroom (unless the dressing room served as an occasional one but it has no closet). The quality of the Purbrook interiors is suggested by Malton's view of the hall (Plate 51). This opened directly onto a columned atrium, lit from above, perhaps the first re-creation of a Roman atrium in England – giving the impression, in Malton's view at least, that it might be an outdoor courtyard and anticipating the Greek Revival halls at Belsay in Northumberland and Millichope in Shropshire. The atrium in turn opened directly onto a semicircular staircase which presumably led up to a landing around the first floor of the atrium, with perhaps a second order of columns. Though the staircase was at one side, and could have been lit by a window in an outside wall – the normal 18th century arrangement – Taylor appears to have lit his staircase purely from above, leaving space for a characteristic vaulted corridor behind. This sense of flow – of a hall opening into an atrium, and the atrium into the staircase, with no intervening walls or doors – was something new in Taylor's houses, and indeed in English architecture, and appears again in Taylor's last villa, Sharpham.[24]

According to Burke's *Visitations of Seats* (1852) Sharpham was 'said to have been commenced *circa* 1770 by Captain Philemon Pownoll from designs by Sir Robert Taylor but was completed by his grandson John Bastard'. Once again the style confirms Taylor's authorship.

Sharpham differs from the other villas as it was a villa on three sides only, attached at the back to an earlier house which contains kitchens, offices and lesser bedrooms. This was perhaps a response to the site as much as to any requirements of Captain Pownoll for Sharpham stands on a spur of land which the Dart winds round in a majestic S-bend. It is a magnificent site; the ground falls away steeply on three sides; more than ever Taylor has chosen a site to see and be seen (Plate 52). As a result the entrance front and the garden front are one, and the house stands in a broad circular ha-ha similar to that shown on the 1840 tithe map at Chute.

Apart from its spectacular position the beauty of Sharpham today is the superb quality of the ashlar facing (Plate 53), heralding that obsession with plain but perfect masonry that is the hallmark of much neoclassical architecture. The columned porch, restrained but more ambitious than the entrances to the earlier villas, opens into an octagonal hall inset with a circular Doric colonnade – each column carrying its own fragment of entablature (Plate 54). The stone paved floor is laid in the pattern of a sixteen-point compass, announcing Pownoll's naval background. The hall opens directly into the staircase hall which has a fair claim to be one of the most breathtaking staircases of any date in England (Plate 56). As at Purbrook one space flows into the other with no door between (Plate 54).

In the staircase hall the floor is once again inscribed with a figurative motif, this time of the architect rather than the owner, with an outline of the geometry by which Taylor's oval took its shape – a central diamond with circles on its points to which two larger circles are added on the long axis. Normally ovals are based on overlapping or abutting circles. By using this method Taylor created a dramatically extended oval but one which did not have flattened sides as a result.

The flight up to the first floor is neatly punctuated on the axis of the front door by a small landing where the balustrade is inset with a panel of crossed Ps for Philemon Pownoll. The real drama is created by the continuous flight from the first to the second floor of thirty-five steps uninterrupted by any landing. Above this the dome rises directly from the oval cylinder of the hall with coffering narrowing towards a large central skylight. It is not only sheer size which makes the Sharpham staircase perhaps the most dramatic of all hanging staircases. Taylor has additionally eliminated all visible means of support – the usual brackets supporting the landings (deriving from those in the Queen's House at Greenwich) are missing. The balustrade similarly is slender and light and nowhere are there stronger newel posts to reinforce the banisters. In the oval staircases of early houses Taylor had placed domes on colonnades or pendentives; here at Sharpham he reduces the structure to the simplest possible geometrical volume: the walls form a cylinder surmounted directly by a dome, showing a concern with elemental forms akin to that of French neoclassical architects like Boullée and Ledoux. On the first floor there is an octagonal saloon in the centre and above this one further conceit – a pair of twin oval bedrooms as at Harleyford and Asgill. Here, however, Taylor resolved the problem of the awkward spaces at either end in an unusually ingenious way: he placed two smaller ovals, a vestibule and a dressing room, in the spaces at right angles to the larger ones (Plate 55). Four ovals were thus inscribed within an octagon, a piece of planning without precedent or sequel.[25]

4 London houses

Malton's plates of Taylor's work include just two London buildings apart from the Bank of England – a banking house at 70 Lombard Street built for Sir Charles Asgill and Ely House in Dover Street for Bishop Edmund Keene of Ely. To these Walpole in his obituary adds 'the duke of Grafton's in Piccadilly' and also notes that 'Mr Gowers near the South Sea house was his first work'.[1] An assiduous correspondent pointed out quickly in the letters column of the *Gentleman's Magazine*[2] that the house was in fact for John Gore of Bush Hill, one of the disqualified directors of the South Sea Company, who, 'being a man of very fair character ... obtained an act, reversing his attainder'. The house was shut off from the street and only visible from the passage between South Sea House and Broad Street. The sole record is an outline elevation in Tallis's *London Street Views* (1838–40) which shows a plain four-storey house with arches or bows on either side of a front door, suggesting it was a business house as well as a residence.

Of these four buildings only Ely House survives and that considerably altered internally in 1909. However, research over a number of years has considerably increased the number of houses which can be confidently ascribed to Taylor, including the very fine houses at 3–6 Grafton Street which as a group are hardly excelled in London. However, it is with two houses at 35–36 Lincoln's Inn Fields (then known as Portugal Row) that Taylor springs upon London architecture, like Athene from the head of Zeus, fully armed and mature.

No. 35 was tragically destroyed by bombing in 1941 but fortunately is well recorded in a 1912 volume of the *Survey of London*.[3] No. 36 was rebuilt in 1859. However, an 1813 view of the Surgeons' College next door shows they were originally built as a matching pair, ingeniously forming one composition. The

Survey of London photograph of 35 (Plate 64) shows that both were approached by a single flight of steps dividing into two, leaving a window bay between the two doors. This was treated like the central bay of No. 35 with a pedimented window on the first floor. Plain and pedimented windows thus must have alternated across the two houses. The uneven number of windows, seven in all, suggests that one house must be considerably larger than the other; Taylor ingeniously evened out the floor area by building the party wall with an S-bend in the middle. At No. 35 this allowed him to win space for a staircase of generous proportions (Plate 68) without having to make the back room narrower than the front, as is usual in London terrace houses. What happened at 36 we do not know.

Externally 35 has the hallmarks of Taylor's style familiar from his villas: the astylar treatment, the triple arcade on the entrance floor, the repeated string courses and the characteristic octagonal glazing. The house is also unusually tall, its four main storeys rising well above its early eighteenth-century neighbour on the left and it was presumably to 35 and 36 that Noorthouck refers in his *History of London* (1773) when describing Lincoln's Inn Fields: 'two in particular on the south side seem to strain at a proud exaltation above all the buildings in the neighbourhood; and are by no means calculated for asthmatic or gouty inhabitants'. In addition there was a well lit basement and an attic storey behind the parapet.

The rear elevation (Plate 65) was also interesting with round headed windows, what might be termed an astylar version of a Palladian window, and a Diocletian window above – such as Taylor used at Harleyford (Plate 25). Other details worth noting are the stepping back of the façade to give a sense of modulation and the pediment on the end of the projecting leg at the back of the house, forming a central feature to both houses – a very superior version of the usual back additions of terrace houses.

Complaints by Scavanger that 'he cannot possibly keep the Fields clean' as a result of building operations suggest that the houses may have been begun in 1754 while in February 1755 there is specific reference to 'workmen employed in building the houses in Portugal Row'. In 1757 Sir Thomas Sewell appears in the rate book for 35 and Sir Anthony Thomas Abdy at 36.[4]

Internally the architectural sophistication of the house is immediately announced in the hall (Plate 66), which is domed and apsed like the hall at Harleyford (Plate 27). The plan suggests, however, that the half dome immediately inside the front door faced the entrance rather than the inner apse. As outside, the treatment here is astylar: there are no pilasters or columns, simply the subtle modulations found at the back of the house. The vestibule opened directly onto an oval staircase, here in the form of two semicircles with a straight section between them. While the early villas had wooden Chinese Chippendale stair rails, 35 Lincoln's Inn Fields has an exceptionally fine wrought-iron balustrade, still very baroque in feeling and reminiscent of Tijou's work in the early part of the century. The ironwork is in a lyre pattern with foliage riveted and welded onto the bars, while on the first-floor landing is a handsome monogrammed panel.

The plans show that both ground and first floors had a sequence of three interconnecting rooms. The ground-floor front room had a coved ceiling with wall niches formed in recessed piers very much like those Taylor used at Coptfold. The middle room has the highly architectural treatment of the libraries in the early villas with blind arches on the walls matching the arches of the windows and shallow square and round panels inset into the frieze zone above (Plate 69). The architectural treatment reaches its climax at the back, where the inside wall had a screen of columns supporting a vaulted ceiling, while the other three walls had a matching Venetian arch motif taking up most of the wall space (Plate 70). This restless determination to articulate every part of the interior with elements of the Orders has the hallmarks of an architect at the beginning of his career determined to secure maximum effect and not too concerned with the consequent problems of arranging furniture and hanging pictures. Here the richness is increased by the fluting of the pilasters, the ornamental detail of both architrave and cornice immediately above, and the egg and dart moulding on the arches and roundels.

The chimney-piece in this room, though rococo in detail, is again of a form that looks back to the early eighteenth century, with a landscape panel inset with an oval mirror. Another playful touch is provided by the scrolls, which take the form of serpents – usually associated with medicine and doctors but present here perhaps as the emblem of logic more appropriate to a lawyer. On the first floor the layout was the same, with a very pretty and delicate rococo ceiling in the front room. This has two other features of interest: a marble chimney-piece with female herms (akin to one in 3 Grafton Street) and a very emphatic door-case with fluted half columns and pediment leading into the middle room – a motif Taylor frequently used both outside and inside. The middle room has one of Taylor's characteristic rococo chimney-pieces which often (understandably) were taken to be of French origin but which correspond very closely to Taylor's fireplace designs in the Taylorian. The room at the back (Plate 67) again has a screen of columns with based vaulted sides and cross-vaulted centre. Here as in many Taylor interiors both skirting and chair rail were richly detailed.

About 1756 Taylor designed a banking house for his friend Sir Charles Asgill.[5] This stood on the site of a tavern known as the White House frequented by Pepys before the Great Fire. The outside was treated very much like a domestic house with the exception of the ground floor, which had a Roman Doric order complete with triglyphs and metopes (Plate 7). Taylor put his stamp on the building by the use of rustication – vermiculated for the low 'pedestal' containing windows lighting the basement and plain rusticated arches around the windows and door. Taylor's treatment is significant as it was to become the standard fascia of banking houses over nearly two centuries. The motif of a ground floor with columns and entablature below and plainer treatment above is familiar from branch banks in almost every town in Britain, providing a bank not only with appropriate *gravitas* at street level but with a comforting domestic feel above. About 1783 Asgill's banking house was acquired by the Pelican (subsequently the Phoenix) Assurance Company and a handsome sculptural group now in the grounds of the Geffrye Museum was added over the entrance. This was executed in London stone from models designed by Lady Diana Beauclerc and portrays Britannia with arm upraised, wielding a standard surmounted by a pelican, giving succour to victims of fire. At some time during the nineteenth century round-headed windows were introduced on the ground floor. *The Builder* in 1915 notes that the Phoenix was 'happy in possessing such architectural offices' and recommended it as worthy of attention from young students. It was not to be for long as the building was subsequently demolished.

Some time before 1767 Taylor built a house for himself at 34 Spring Gardens. It is tantalising that the only visual record of it should be a partial glimpse of the exterior in a photograph taken in 1903.[6] From the obituary in the *London Chronicle* it is clear that it was of altogether exceptional interest, architecturally aspiring to rival Soane's house in Lincoln's Inn Fields or Burgess's in Melbury Road, Kensington: 'The house in Spring Gardens is a great curiosity for the economy of space, fanciful shapes and multiplied accommodations ... there is scarcely anything so pretty in London. Foreigners should see it.'[7] *The Builder* in 1846 adds a little more:[8]

> The house, now No. 34, occupied as the private residence of Mr Barrack, the owner of the adjoining hotel, remains for the most part as Sir Robert left it, and withinside displays an artistical feeling, exhibited by a greater sacrifice of room and convenience than we should now be willing to make. The principal apartments are octagonal or circular in plan; the staircase is also of the latter form, and is adorned with heads from the antique on brackets.

Spring Gardens took its name from the Spring Garden formed, it is thought, in the reign of Queen Elizabeth in the north-east corner of St James's Park as an addition to the pleasure grounds of Whitehall Palace. There was at least one house in Spring Garden as early as 1635 and building continued during the Commonwealth. The development of Spring Gardens as a fashionable residential street was mainly a mid-eighteenth-century phenomenon, following which for nearly a century it was inhabited principally by politicians and civil servants. From 1853 onwards more and more of Spring Gardens was acquired for Admiralty purposes and most of the site was cleared in 1885. The new Admiralty building was completed in 1891 and a further block by Aston Webb, including Admiralty Arch, was opened in 1910.

In 1767–8 Taylor substantially remodelled No. 33 Upper Brook Street, which still survives.[9] The work was carried out for Sir John Boyd, Bt, for whom Taylor had built Danson in Kent. It was probably a speculation as in 1769 Sir Henry Houghton, 6th Baronet, MP (1728–95)[10], moved in. Houghton again had characteristic links: his second wife Fanny, whom he married in 1766, was the daughter and co-heiress of a director of the Bank of England, Daniel Booth, while in 1768 he had stood jointly for Preston with General John Burgoyne, who built 3 Grafton Street for Lord Howe and almost certainly used Taylor as architect for the ballroom he added at The Oaks, Carshalton (Plate 63).

A note in the rate books in 1768 stating that the rates were paid by 'Mr Taylor in Spring Gardens'[11] provides documentary evidence that Taylor was the architect, and this is amply confirmed by stylistic parallels with other houses. Outside, No. 33 is characteristically astylar, but it has the triple arched arcade found at Harleyford, Chute, 35 Lincoln's Inn Fields and later at Ely House in Dover Street. The original pediment, however, has been absorbed in a full attic storey at third-floor level. Taylor placed the front door centrally, rather than at the side as is usual; it opened into a vestibule carrying his characteristic cross-vaults and a central dome opening on the left through a screen of columns onto a cantilevered stair. The arches carrying the vaults and dome were typically inlaid with a guilloche pattern. The back of the house at both ground- and first-floor levels was fully taken up by a large octagonal room similar to those at Danson and Asgill. A drawing of the first-floor room in 1810 shows a faithful version of the famous octagonal coffered ceiling illustrated in Robert Wood's *Ruins of Palmyra* (1753), variants of which Taylor used in 3 and 6 Grafton Street.

Some considerable compensation for the loss of Taylor's house in Spring Gardens comes with the survival of a group of four houses designed by him in Grafton Street, Nos 3–6 (Plate 71). These have been attributed to Taylor for some time on stylistic grounds but documentary evidence makes it clear they were part of a larger group of at least fourteen houses all built to Taylor's designs between 1768 and 1775 on the west and north sides of Grafton Street, which unusually is in the form of an L connecting Dover Street with New Bond Street.[12]

Mention of new buildings in Grafton Street comes in the vestry minutes of St George's Hanover Square on 26 January 1768: 'Vestry Clerk waited on Mr Taylor, architect and surveyor to the

Duke of Grafton touching the stoppage of the highway from Bond Street to Dover Street . . . Ordered that Mr Taylor be desired to attend with the plan of the intended buildings.' A year later, on 20 January 1769, the Clerk of the Westminster Commissioners of Sewers also mentions 'Mr Taylor the architect and Mr Gray the builder, of the several new houses at Hay Hill', acting with 'orders from his Grace the Duke of Grafton to whom the Ground belonged'.[13]

The rate books show the progress of the project.[14] Three houses were occupied in 1771, seven in 1772 and twelve in 1774. The rate books, as usual at this date, do not give the numbers of the houses but these are given on Richard Horwood's map of London (1792–9) and with the help of Boyle's *Court Guide* of 1792 and a sale catalogue of 1812[15] it is possible to identify the original occupants of the individual houses. From all this it emerges that Nos 1–6 and 7–14 round the corner were built with one possible exception by 1775.

The earliest glimpses of the houses come in two views of Hay Hill in 1806 which show No. 1, whose first occupant was Sir George Warren.[16] The houses are externally plain with little in the way of architectural dressing apart from handsome Tuscan doorcases. Rather they have a look of eighteenth-century houses in Dublin, for example in Henrietta Street where there is the same mixture of broad plain brick fronts three or four windows wide, with only the distance between the first and second floor windows giving a hint of the very grand rooms within.

Around the corner Taylor gave alternate houses a two-storey bay window (Plate 77), like the canted bays of his villas, another instance of him introducing a feature that was to become a commonplace feature of nineteenth- and early twentieth-century terrace houses all over the country.

Nos 1 and 2 were rebuilt at the turn of the century but No. 3, built for Lord Howe, survives though dramatically altered by Mrs Arthur James early this century.[17] The building lease among the Grafton papers in the Suffolk Record Office shows, as mentioned earlier, that General Burgoyne built Admiral Howe's house for him and specifies plans and elevations settled and from time to time approved by the Duke of Grafton, adding that 'the whole work shall be done under the direction of Robert Taylor'.

The agreement was for 'a substantial dwelling house of the best brick stone and other materials fit for the habitations of gentlemen' and the house was to be completed in three years (which it was, according to the first rate of building). In addition it was stipulated that 'no part of the said House shall be made into a shop or shops or have any Mark or show of Business whatsoever' – restrictions such as later governed the development of Belgravia.

With this is a contract between Burgoyne and the builders and craftsmen involved. These were Edward Gray of Queen Street, Grosvenor Square (Taylor's usual builder), James Swinton of Greenwich, carpenter, and Henry Barell of St Martin-in-the-Fields, mason and carver.

The alterations made by Mrs James earlier this century incorporated and also modified much of the original work so it is difficult to unravel the two. The main feature of the house today is an impressive top-lit imperial staircase. This has the cantilevered stone flights characteristic of Taylor and a beautiful S-pattern iron balustrade (Plate 73) almost identical to that in No. 4 next door (Plate 74), though with the added touch of an extra decorative panel between the S-panels. The drawing room ceiling is also identical to the ceiling of one of the first-floor rooms in No. 6, both being a variant of the famous coffered ceiling at Palmyra. The chimney-piece in this room with pairs of female herms is like one at 35 Lincoln's Inn Fields. Another feature which speaks of Taylor is the screen in the form of a Venetian arch with the inner arch encircled in an outer one: the same motif as found at the Bank of England.[18]

No. 4 Grafton Street survives virtually intact, and has recently been excellently restored by a major international company. This house was built for Lord Villiers and first appears in the rate books in 1775 at £210.[19] Lord Villiers's house was built to entertain on a grand scale: Mrs Montagu in her *Ladies of the Last Century* describes Villiers as 'the Prince of Maccaronies'.[20] He was a great friend of the Duke of Grafton, while Fox in a letter of 1762 states that 'Lord Villiers will be entirely guided by Lord Spencer', for whom Taylor also worked at Althorp and Spencer House. His sumptuous London house may well have been prompted by his marriage in 1770 to Frances, the posthumous daughter and sole heiress of Philip Twysden, the Bishop or Raphoe in Ireland.

The house has a particularly handsome entrance vestibule (Plate 72), recently repaved in stone, with a cross-vault springing from pairs of Doric columns carrying sections of full entablature. By contrast to the hall at 35 Lincoln's Inn Fields, where the concentration of architectural elements in a small space was almost overwhelming, Taylor here aims at a much greater lightness. This is achieved partly by a greater expanse of bare wall: the entablature is confined to the columns; there is no dado, and skirting is as simple as can be. The same striving for lightness is seen in the screen between hall and staircase with a great segmental fanlight filling the arch and only the slenderest of iron glazing bars. The screen, it is interesting to note, does not carry a full entablature but only a simple cornice (unlike the columns in the vestibule) and this meant Taylor committed the solecism, in grammatical terms, of juxtaposing two columns of the same order but of different height and proportions. Amidst the elegance of the whole this is likely to pass unnoticed – an architectural equivalent of the new lightness Robert Adam was introducing in plasterwork. The staircase beyond is of rare elegance and drama, the London counterpart of Taylor's great staircase hall at Sharpham, and a rival indeed to Kent's renowned staircase at 44 Berkeley Square. Walls are again virtually bare of ornament and with the light flooding in from the dome above all structural detail is almost burnt out and the balustrade appears suspended in the air. As usual, the lightness is further increased by cutting away the underside of each tread and as at Sharpham the first-floor landing is without any supporting brackets. The staircase only ascends to the first floor but at second-floor level there is a gallery on ¾ sides providing access to different rooms (Plate 74). It is interesting that here Taylor gradually introduces more ornamental detail – a frieze zone of inset panels, an enriched architrave, and brackets supporting the landing. Above the treatment becomes more ornamental still with delicate Adamesque plasterwork in the spandrels and an intricately detailed cornice carrying the dome.

On the ground floor there are two main rooms set end to end. That at the back is the most elaborate room in the terrace (Plate

75), similar in treatment to the room Taylor added at The Oaks, Carshalton, for General John Burgoyne (Plate 63). Pairs of unusually short Corinthian columns carry a rich entablature supporting a blind arcade of three arches to each wall. Over the chimney-piece and around the walls are a series of circular medallions – a refinement of the plain roundels of the earlier houses. The first-floor apartment does not consist only of the usual two rooms set end to end, but also has an anteroom over the entrance hall with a segmented vaulted ceiling; this is ornamented with a delicate pattern of interlocking circles, half of each circle being metamorphosed into a trail of leaves. At the back is another highly architectural room – perhaps a form of cabinet with large segmental apses springing from pairs of pilasters (Plate 76). Here only a simplified version of the cornice is carried round the room, again lightening the overall effect. As this room is accessible directly from the secondary stair it may have been used for business.

No. 5 Grafton Street was first occupied by Arnold Nesbitt in 1772. This again has a very elegant stair, here continuing to the second floor, with a balustrade similar to No. 4's but slightly simpler. Here too Taylor creates a sense that the dome floats above the walls, this time by reducing to the barest minimum the cornice and brackets from which it springs. In the hall of No. 5 is a very fine stone chimney-piece with a naturalistic frieze carved for an owner who clearly enjoyed his wine – groups of putti harvest the grapes while their elders grow tipsy on the results. The carving is suggestive of the manner of Sir Henry Cheere and may be a late sculptural design by Taylor, who of course had begun as Cheere's apprentice. Other fine features in this house are a pair of doors and door-cases moved in about 1900 from No. 3.

The last house in this group is No. 6, which is something of an enigma as it does not appear in the rate books till 1786, when it is rated at £130 for two years under Michael Barrett (who is entered as owning at least three houses for short periods). In 1793 Robert Thornton, an East India Company director, moved in. The explanation for this delay is probably that No. 6 was on an awkward site, much shallower than its neighbours. Taylor overcame this with some ingenuity. The house has a wide front with a central entrance leading into a coffered and barrel-vaulted entrance vestibule. Here it was not possible to place the staircase on the axis of the front door as in Nos 4 and 5 and Taylor had to introduce a kink or slant at the end of the vestibule which leads to a spacious staircase opening off to the left. On the first floor are two handsome intercommunicating rooms, one of these has a Palmyra ceiling as found in No. 3.

All the houses round the corner have now been demolished, though No. 7, well known today as the home of the Medici Gallery, does incorporate some of Taylor's work. The existing street front appears to be built on the eighteenth-century basement vaults which are similar to Taylor's work elsewhere, while behind survives, somewhat altered, what must have been Taylor's staircase in the shape of a D, with the landings on the inner straight side and the stairs rising round the curve and lit by a Palladian window.

Fortunately a full photographic record was made by the Greater London Council of No. 14 before it was demolished (Plate 77). This first appears in 1772 as the home of John Stewart and from then on under Mrs Stewart. Though the house was somewhat smaller than those round the corner, the treatment was still highly architectural, with one of Taylor's characteristic cross-vaulted vestibules (Plate 78). Each compartment, as usual, is divided by a cross-rib inset with a guilloche pattern, here of alternating large and small circles. The hall leads directly to an oval staircase, more compact than those in Nos 4 and 5, but with a plain railing of great simplicity and elegance.

An idea of the way these houses were used is provided by a sale catalogue of July 1812 which has a full description of No. 9, whose first resident was Sir John Taylor. On the ground floor there was an entrance hall with a 'vaulted roof' (as at No. 14), a stone staircase which ran from the basement to the second floor (not just the first as in No. 4), 'a capital dining parlour', a 'library communicating' and a porter's room. On the first floor was a 'handsome lofty drawing-room in front' with marble chimney-pieces and papered walls, communicating with 'a Breakfast Parlour correspondingly finished'.[21] Both ground and first floors contained what are today called reception rooms. The bedrooms were on the second floor — 'three excellent bed-chambers, with closets' — and above them 'four very commodious servants' rooms'. In the basement was a 'housekeeper's room fitted up with closets, etc., and chambers adjoining', a water closet, butler's pantry and a 'very capital commodious and lofty kitchen, fitted up with dressers, shelves, etc.' As in Taylor's villas the kitchen here was evidently given greater ceiling height than adjoining rooms, while in addition there was 'a scullery, with water laid on, coal holes, laundry, servants' hall, and cellars for wine, beer, etc.' Though this sale catalogue dates from thirty years after the houses were finished, the likelihood is that the arrangement was the original one.

The best known of Taylor's London houses is Ely House[22] in Dover Street, long familiar as the London home of Oxford University Press (Plate 79). Most of the original houses in Dover Street had been built between about 1686 and 1710. The predecessor of No. 37 had been acquired in 1715 by the Chetwynd family who occupied it until 1772 when Esther Chetwynd sold the property for £5,600 to Edmund Keene, Bishop of Ely. As Taylor often acted for his patrons in purchasing sites, he may well have been led to the choice of this particular site by his connection with the Chetwynd family – his best church monument is the statue in Grendon Church Warwick to Miss Mary Chetwynd, who died in 1750 aged ninety-one.[23]

Taylor had already worked for Bishop Keene remodelling the Bishop's Palace at Chester, and carrying out alterations at the Bishop's Palace at Ely soon after Keene's appointment to the see in 1771. Keene's own introduction may have come from his wife, the heiress of a retired Cheshire linen-draper, Lancelot Andrews of Edmonton. They had married in May 1753[24] and Lancelot Andrews was a neighbour of John Gore of Edmonton, the former South Sea Company director who had given Taylor his first commission at 112 Bishopsgate within.

Keene's own background was a business one. His father was a mercer and alderman of King's Lynn while his elder brother, Sir Benjamin Keene MP (*c.* 1697–1757), had been sent to Madrid at an early age as agent of the South Sea Company,[25] later becoming consul, minister and ambassador there in succession. Walpole's high opinion of Benjamin Keene had undoubtedly played a part in Edmund Keene's meteoric rise at Cambridge University, where he became vice-chancellor at the age of twenty five.

The old London Palace of the Bishops of Ely had stood since the end of the thirteenth century on the north side of Holborn, near Gray's Inn. In 1576 the Bishops had been constrained to lease most of the front courtyard to Elizabeth's favourite and Lord Chancellor Sir Christopher Hatton and this divided ownership had continued until the death of the last Lord Hatton in 1762, when the Hatton property reverted to the Crown. In 1772 by a special Act of Parliament the see of Ely transferred all its rights in the site and buildings to the Crown for £6,500, an annuity of £200, and the sum of £5,600 to purchase the freehold in Dover Street, by then a much more fashionable and accessible London base for the bishops.

The rate books show the premises as empty for four years until Taylor's new house was completed in 1776. Taylor's façade was described by Christopher Hussey as 'a masterpiece of street architecture' in an excellent short monograph, *The Story of Ely House*, produced for the Consolidated Zinc Corporation in 1953. 'The problem posed to architects', he wrote, 'by the designing of a narrow front that shall at once be self-contained and yet part of the street's elevation, has seldom if ever been solved in such a satisfactory manner.' Taylor achieved this sense of containment by the subtle way he handled the junction of his front with his neighbours. His elegant ashlar front does not just abut the two adjoining buildings. Instead, at ground-floor level there is a tiny recess between the buildings (Plate 80), allowing Taylor to turn the rustication round the corner. Above, the first and second floors have a double return, suggesting to the eye, in Christopher Hussey's words, 'that the house has sides, running back from the street'. The double return also allows just enough space for the full cornice to be carried round at right angles.

The overall effect at the front is of a restrained elegance, appropriate to a bishop, though it was later to excite the wrath of Pugin.[26] As usual Taylor eschews the use of an order or a pediment in contrast, say, to Stuart's exquisite ashlar front of a decade earlier at 15 St James's Square. Though this was the only one of Taylor's London houses to be of stone rather than brick, the characteristic hallmarks appear – the triple arcade, the vermiculated rustication (which he made increasingly forceful use of in the 1770s) and the aedicule motif of columns and pediment to the first floor windows, which he usually used as a front door. Though today it may seem a palatial residence for a bishop, by comparison with medieval bishops' palaces it was a typical town residence, only the bishop's hat in the central roundel proclaiming its clerical owner.

The interior of the house was greatly altered when it was enlarged and adapted for the Ladies' Albermarle Club in 1909. The finest feature was the staircase, similar to that at No. 4 Grafton Street, originally rising only to the first floor with a gallery at second floor level. The balustrade is virtually identical in every detail but the dome resting on short barrel vaults at either end and carried on pairs of pilasters is just a little more richly detailed (Plate 81).

The Architectural Publications Society's *Dictionary* mentions a house by Taylor in 'Whitehall Yard (?Lord Carrington's)' for which there is no other documentation. This could simply be a confusion with Carrington House in Whitehall Yard which was built by Sir William Chambers in 1765–74 for the second Lord Gower. However *The World* of 4 July 1788 mentions that Sir Robert Taylor has just bought Lady Townsend's house in Whitehall. Shortly after Taylor's death there is a further report on 24 October that Mr Taylor (Sir Robert's son, Michelangelo) 'begins immediately on his new home in Whitehall. The old building of Lady Townsend's he pulls down, and according to a plan of Sir Robert's he raises a house which will be one of the best in London.'

Some details of the house, now demolished, are given in the *Survey of London*.[27] In 1788 the existing house was described as in 'so decayed a state as to be scarcely habitable' but apparently rebuilding did not begin until 1793. Over the next ten years the north half was reconstructed 'in a most substantial manner, and the other part stripped to the walls, and entirely refitted and raised two storeys higher'. Externally the house is plain with an arcade at ground floor level; within, it had an elegant cantilevered stone staircase similar to the Grafton Street houses. On the basis of surviving evidence it seems possible that the design was indeed Sir Robert Taylor's but modified in execution by a pupil.

5   Public works

Soon after his turn to architecture, Taylor received an exotic and unusual public commission: to design a Lord Mayor's Coach for his friend Sir Charles Asgill.[1] The study of state coaches is a fascinating subject best pursued in the famous coach museum in Lisbon and through Rudolf Wackernagel's impressive monograph, *Die Französische Kronüngswagen* (Berlin 1966). In England pride of place naturally goes to the superb Royal State Coach designed by Sir William Chambers in 1760 and first used by George III at the opening of Parliament in November 1762. In terms of craftsmanship and finish the Royal Coach is undoubtedly the finer, but the Lord Mayor's has precedence in terms of date. And while the Royal Coach is stylistically a harbinger of neoclassicism Taylor's is best described as the apotheosis of the rococo – rarely in England was the rococo abhorrence of straight lines and right angles given such three-dimensional effect.

The coach was formally commissioned on 4 April 1757 and was ready for the Lord Mayor's procession in November the same year. The procession dated back to 1115, when King John gave a charter to the City, attaching the condition that the Mayor would present himself for approval by the King or his sheriff each year at Westminster before taking office. The custom of going by water to Westminster began about 1422; for the landward part of the journey the Lord Mayor went on horseback until 1711, when a coach was hired for the first time. The recurring problem of hiring led the aldermen to commission a coach of their own. Each alderman agreed to subscribe £60 and to pay a further £100 to the repair of the coach as and when he became Lord Mayor. The agreement for the building of the 'New Grand State Coach' was made with Joseph Berry of Leather Lane, Holborn, who had been master of the Coachmakers' Company in 1749. For an agreed fixed price of £860 he undertook to 'finish and compleate' the coach 'exactly to the model made thereof by Mr Robert Taylor'. Both the design and the detail of the coach suggest inspiration from Parisian models. There is a close parallel with the so called *Goldene Wagen* built for the solemn entry of the Imperial Ambassador to the French Court, Fürst Joseph Wenzel von Liechtenstein, into Paris on 31 December 1738. This appears to have been built after a design of Nicholas Pineau's, whose work Taylor would have known in engravings.

On the Lord Mayor's Coach the coachman's seat is supported by two twisting merfolk (inspired perhaps by Bernini's triton fountain in Rome); his foot-rest is an expressionistically carved scallop shell. At the back, the hindcarriage is in the form of an open cartouche with a swan below (shades of Ludwig of Bavaria's swan coach), with two putti (one a merboy) acting as supporters to a shield bearing the City's arms. Two fire-breathing dragons perch on the extruded corners of the frame. The painted panels on the sides and back of the coach have been attributed to G. B. Cipriani (1727–85).

The great public work of Taylor's career was his series of extensions of the Bank of England.[2] 'The magnificent additions to the Bank', Walpole wrote, 'are his grandest work. And these, when a foreigner of the first taste, M. de Calonne, saw them, he pronounced them, with no exception but St Paul's, the first architecture in London.' Taylor's work, already much reduced by Soane's alterations, was almost wholly eliminated by Sir Herbert Baker in his rebuilding in 1921–37. And, though Baker recreated Taylor's masterpiece, his Court Room, in a new position, he simplified, altered and even eliminated much of Taylor's exquisitely delicate detail. That the room still looks imposing is therefore all the more a tribute to the strength of Taylor's design.

Taylor's appointment at the Bank is usually said to date from 1765 but he is already mentioned as the Bank's Surveyor in March 1764 and in November that year as architect to the Bank. Taylor was not the Bank's first architect. In 1731 a committee had been appointed at the Bank to consider two sets of plans for a new building by Henry Joynes (*c.* 1684–1754) and George Sampson (d. ?1764). Neither plan was considered satisfactory and advice was sought from Theodore Jacobsen (d. 1772), later the designer of the Foundling Hospital. Jacobsen took the opportunity to present his own scheme, a variant of Colen Campbell's Stourhead, dating from a decade earlier, and on 19 August the Court of Directors resolved to thank Jacobsen 'for the great pains and troubles he hath taken in revising the several plans for a new Bank, and to desire the continuation of his assistance in fixing a plan for the building intended to be erected'. In the event the new buildings seem to have been built to Sampson's designs (Plate 8). A contract was let in 1732 but final payments were not made till 1743, by which time a total of £18,194 0s 4d had been spent.

Sampson's building, laid out around two courts, was soon outgrown, and in 1751 there is a reference to an allowance of £5,891 17s 10d made by the Treasury for further offices. In March 1764 an Act of Parliament was passed to allow the directors to purchase land to the east of Sampson's façade up to the corner of Bartholomew Lane, and to buy the buildings in front of the Bank, between Threadneedle Street and Cornhill, 'for opening up a passage for carriages from Cornhill to the Bank,[3] and for building houses on either side', and incidentally opening up an axial view of Sampson's façade.

Taylor's first work for the Bank was Bank Buildings, two blocks on either side of the new axial approach, dramatically portrayed in a painting by William Marlow (Plate 8). A contract was signed with the builder Edward Gray in October 1764 and building must have progressed rapidly as the first lease to the Sun Fire Office dates from 1766. The Bank Buildings were demolished in 1844 to make way for Tite's Royal Exchange (part of the site became an open space in front of his portico). Taylor's ingenious planning on an awkward site was praised by Cockerell in his Royal Academy lectures.[4] Taylor had contrived no less than nine staircases, several of them characteristically in oval or circular wells. Shortly after, in 1847, the *Civil Engineer and Architects' Journal*[5] praised Bank Buildings as 'a masterpiece of street architecture, putting situation aside, not surpassed by any in Europe'. The anonymous author was particularly impressed by Taylor's attached colonnade 'of as elegant a Roman-Doric as ever emanated from the pencil of a modern architect'. The intercolumniations, he added, were filled with doors and windows as necessity and internal convenience required, 'deeply recessed and with bold reveals that served for every purpose of office or shop'. In this way Taylor gave unity to the whole block by a continuous applied order surmounted by a balustrade, but allowed complete flexibility in terms of the uses within. Above this, the *Civil Engineer* notes the well proportioned windows 'with that breadth between them which characterises all this architect's works'. Bank Buildings have an added interest as the precursor of the engaging triangular blocks of shops and offices built along Queen Victoria Street when it was cut through the existing grid of streets in 1867–71.

Taylor's plans for the new offices to the east of Sampson's façade were approved by the directors in March 1765 and on 1 January 1768 the *London Chronicle* recorded that 'the several offices were opened'.

Taylor's new block was treated externally with a screen wall without any windows or openings (Plate 8) apart from a secondary entrance half-way along Bartholomew's Lane. Its design has been deprecated in the past as eclectic – as a plagiarism of Bramante's Belvedere courtyard in the Vatican, where the arcade has the same repeating triumphal arch motif. However, a knowledgeable writer in the 1846 *Civil Engineer* pinpointed the source more exactly: '. . . he found a pretty design for a tetrastyle portico and pediment, with lateral columns of a very elegantly-proportioned Corinthian order raised upon pedestals, in Chambers' work on "Civil Architecture", confessedly borrowed from an anonymous Italian architect'.

Taylor made his new site square by giving up some ground to public use. Within, the additions consisted of an oval vestibule leading into a circular exchange with four transfer offices opening off them (Plate 9). Again the charge of plagiarism has been laid on Taylor: the domed rotunda (Plate 10) is inspired by the Pantheon in Rome while the idea of columns supporting arches which carry a sequence of smaller domes in the aisles clearly derives from Gibbs's St Martin-in-the-Fields (1722–26). Taylor's treatment, as far as can be judged from Malton's engravings (Plate 11), was altogether lighter: the columns were not anchored to the galleries and, by the introduction of lights into the domes along the aisles, Taylor created a real sense that the whole ceiling is floating. This impression of a hanging ceiling is increased by the playful interlacing pattern of the ribs and the two further domes which rise from the centre of the ceiling without any support from below.

The rotunda is of interest as an early example of an exchange taking the form of a large covered hall[6] – the earlier Royal Exchanges of 1566 and 1667–71 had been designed in the form of quadrangles with arcades surmounted by ranges of rooms around an open court. Taylor's rotunda, by contrast, was the prototype of all the great exchanges in the City – the Stock Exchange, the Coal Exchange (which was on the same circular plan) and the Baltic Exchange – and of numerous exchanges in provincial cities and towns, for example Brodrick's remarkable oval Corn Exchange in Leeds (1861–5). Similarly the Transfer Office with the desks of the clerks ranged around the outer walls anticipated the characteristic form of a banking hall as we know it today, with ranges of counters around an open floor.

Taylor's additions to the west of Sampson's buildings (Plate 9) were carried out in two phases. First came the Court Room and associated offices some way back from Threadneedle Street, and second the construction of a colonnade with offices behind along Threadneedle Street matching the wing Taylor had added to the east. This involved the acquisition and demolition of the Church of St Christopher-Le-Stocks.

The date of the Court Room is usually given as 1774, following H. R. Steele in 1929. In fact Taylor's design can be dated nearly a decade earlier. A report in the *London Chronicle* of 16–18 June 1767 states that 'the new room for the Bank directors and committee is building on the West side of the Bank behind St Christopher's Church'. The land on which it was built was purchased under a special Act of Parliament of 1765, and it is probable that Taylor's first designs date from about this time.

Five years later there is a large settlement in the accounts with John Rose, 'plasterer', for £814 6s 0d and this probably indicates that the work was nearly complete. A drawing survives by Taylor for the room (Plate 12) which must be an early scheme of 1765 if not before, as there is still rococo decoration in the panels inset above the Venetian windows.

The early design, like the finished room (Plate 13), has the screens of columns so approved of by C. R. Cockerell in his

Royal Academy lecture in 1845 – 'the Bank Parlour is one of the most original and scenic in its contrivance, and is peculiar to Sir R. Taylor, as he has shewn at Clumber, in his own house in Spring Gardens as well as at the Bank. That contrivance is that you enter the room by lateral corridores from whence the proportion of the room is entirely enjoyed as it were from an external point of view.'[7] Taylor used this format elsewhere, for example at Braxted (1753–6) and Trewithen (*c.* 1763–4); however, there is at least one example of a similar room of an earlier date at the old hall at Wentworth Woodhouse, dating from *c.* 1725, where there is a screen of three arches at either end resting directly on the capitals of the columns without any intervening entablature.

Cockerell's one criticism was that the 'order is very small, the ceiling is perhaps a little flat and deficient in dignity of relief'. Taylor, however, used these short columns elsewhere, for example at the Oaks, Carshalton (Plate 63), while the low relief of the walls, if not the ceiling, particularly the blind arcade on the inner wall, again has a neoclassical feel, looking towards the shallow modulations of Thomas Hope and Soane. The real virtuosity of the plasterwork is seen inside the arcades (Plate 14), where octagonal coffering is dextrously married with cross-vaulting. The resulting triangular corners had no awkwardness about them and indeed the repeat of the egg-and-tongue moulding around such small panels heightened the richness of the effect.

Taylor provided the Court Room with no less than three chimney-pieces, one in each bay of the inner wall. This in itself seems unique – pairs of fireplaces are quite frequently found in large and important rooms but three so close together is hard to parallel.

The plasterwork is something of a puzzle. Mercury's caduceus, in the corners above the arcade, is to be expected as the symbol of bankers, but the roundels between the arches contain a series of portrait heads in profile of English kings and queens, each framed with laurel wreathes – William and Mary, Anne, the four Georges, William IV and Queen Victoria. The roundels in the ceilings, by contrast, contained small portrait heads of Roman emperors and the letters SPQR. Was this intended as some parallel between Roman emperors and English monarchs, suggesting the splendour of Britain vying with that of Rome? The answer seems to be that these portrait heads were a later introduction perhaps of the imperial mood of the later nineteenth century.

One change between the early design (Plate 12) and the executed scheme was the replacement of the solid panels above the Palladian windows with glass (Plate 15), greatly lightening the effects. Taylor continued this motif around the courtyard – the former churchyard of St Christopher-Le-Stocks. These exquisitely proportioned Venetian windows were much admired by the *Civil Engineer*: 'there is not an executed building of the decorative Greco-Roman style in Europe, that more deserves the title of tasteful and elegant than does this pretty composition of Sir Robert Taylor's'.[8]

The last phase of Taylor's work was prompted by the Gordon Riots of 1780. The Bank directors feared that the church might be stormed by the mob and prove a vantage-point from which to attack the bank, and an Act of Parliament was obtained for its acquisition and demolition. Externally Taylor repeated the blind arcade. The only interior of which we have a record is his Reduced Annuity Office (Plate 16). This is a remarkable design as it directly prefigures Soane's Bank Stock Office of 1792 – which has long been recognised as a major watershed in neoclassicism. Taylor's use of segmental arches springing from clusters of columns with fragments of entablature stems from his hall at 4 Grafton Street (Plate 72) in the early 1770s. The idea for a sidelit dome may have derived from criticisms of his earlier domes in the transfer offices, for Northouck's *History of London* says that the light there had flooded down perpendicularly and as a result 'the reflection from the white papers of the books is too direct to the eyes of the clerks, a circumstance which is much complained of by them'.

The World of 25 June 1787 adds some further details: 'In one of the rooms the light comes from the top – but in a better mode than in the large rooms, sometime since finished – as the window goes round the whole room, and the sashes being *vertical*, half of them open.' The new buildings, it adds, will consist of four rooms and 'will be finished in the course of the year' and 'will well complete the works of Sir Robert Taylor'.

Taylor's other major public commission in London was for Stone Buildings in Lincoln's Inn.[9] On 17 April 1771 the Council of the Society of Lincoln's Inn resolved to commission plans from Robert Adam, James Paine, the younger Brettingham and Taylor. On 12 December there was a further resolution that application should be made only to Taylor, but on 1 June 1772 the Council learnt that Adam, Paine and Wyatt intended to submit plans. Two years later, on 28 July 1774, it was agreed that general approval would be sought for Taylor's plans.

Robert Adam's spectacular scheme was published by A. T. Bolton in the *Architectural Review*, but those by Brettingham and Paine which used to be in the library at Lincoln's Inn have disappeared.[10]

As executed Taylor's plan is unusual among Palladian public buildings in having no central emphasis (Plate 19). Instead it is the ends which break forward and are crowned with pediments rather in the manner of Gabriel's blocks in the Place de la Concorde in Paris. However, a plan in the Ashmolean (Plate 18) shows that Taylor's original scheme was for a building nearly double the length of Stone Buildings today with a projecting centre treated with applied columns – not unlike his scheme for Heveningham. The whole scheme, it has to be admitted, would have been rather monotonous. As it stands, it is nonetheless both eloquent and imposing, the beautifully jointed ashlar of the upper floors set off very effectively by the bold arcades and rustication of the ground floor where each stone is beautifully tooled. Though the interiors are plain the layout is of some considerable interest, consisting of sets of chambers of four rooms, with Taylor's characteristic cross-vaulted vestibules and passages constantly appearing. Each set of chambers is entered through an office with a study, library and bedroom. The ingenious way in which these suites of chambers were worked out with the windows always centrally or symmetrically placed must be a principal reason why Taylor won the commission, reflecting Walpole's praise that 'his plans were free from faults'.[11]

On 18 June 1777 Taylor was paid £262 10s, representing 5 per cent commission on the £5,250 spent on 1 and 2 Stone Buildings, and work continued in 1778 and 1779. The south pavilion was completed in 1842–45 under the direction of P. Hardwick.

Taylor's other building at Lincoln's Inn, the Six Clerks and Enrolment Offices (1775–77),[12] is more original (Plate 20). This is a neoclassical variant on a Palladian theme. Above the usual rusticated ground floor Taylor introduces a giant series of arched windows pressing the attic windows close against the boldly projecting cornice. The design directly anticipates Robert Mylne's Stationers' Hall in London (1800–1), which in Summerson's words shows Mylne 'at his Neo-Classical best'.

While work was continuing at Lincoln's Inn Taylor received the commission for a large new Assembly Room at Belfast. This was to be built on top of the Exchange, erected in 1769 by the fifth Earl of Donegall at a cost of £4,000. According to S. Shannon Miller's *Sidelights on Belfast History* (1932) the Exchange was a single storey building, virtually square in shape in which the principal building traders and merchants met daily to transact business. Seven years later the Earl, (who became first Marquess of Donegall in 1791) added the Assembly Room at a cost of £7,000. Malton's engraving provides the evidence that Taylor was the architect. The room has an Order of pilasters carrying a segmantel coffered vault and characteristic Taylor touches in the roundels with classical reliefs and the plaque or tablet over the central door. Arthur Young in his *Tour of Ireland* (1780) notes the Assembly Room was a double square in plan '60 feet long by 30 feet broad, and 24 feet high'. Adjoining were a Card Room and a Tea Room both of 32 feet by 22 feet. Large first floor halls with shallow barrel vaults were a characteristic of the 1770s and 1780s – other examples were the so called Wagon Room at Brooks's Club St James Street, London by Henry Holland (1776–78) and the dining room at White's across the street, attributed to James Wyatt (1787–88). A miniature version acting as an entrance hall is to be found at Mount Clare, Roehampton (1770) a villa with a canted bay on the garden front.

Two other groups of public commissions deserve discussion – Taylor's bridges and his churches – before we turn to his last work, the Council House at Salisbury. Between 1756 and 1766 Taylor had been responsible for the remodelling of old London

Bridge in collaboration with George Dance senior.[13] Taylor's joint submission with Dance to the committee for improving the bridge is dated 20 July 1756. By 1762, the estimate for completion was £86,550 19s 4d. Taylor and Dance received £3,494 9s. Together they had the unenviable task of removing the houses along the bridge which had always given it such legendary appeal, and of replacing the two central arches by a single arch. Balustrades and parapets were then added along the new widened carriageway. The bridge was demolished in 1831.

The practical resolution of this difficult problem may have led to the commission for Maidenhead bridge, which was built to Taylor's designs between 1772 and 1777, replacing an existing timber bridge.[14] The builder was John Townsend, who contracted to build the bridge for £15,741. This undoubtedly deserves a high place among the many beautiful eighteenth-century bridges. Its special quality lies in the studied elegance of its line – a gentle serpentine, convex as it rises over the river and concave as it falls to meet the land (Plate 17). Here as in so many of his buildings Taylor makes memorable use of vermiculated rustication, emphasising the outline of the arches against the dominant balustrade above. Taylor's drawings fortunately survive – there are a total of just six covering the whole design and all the details, showing his ability to condense information in a highly rational and digestible manner.

With Maidenhead bridge, long known as Taylor's work from Malton's engraving, goes a more recent discovery: that he designed six bridges on the Botley Road at Oxford of which Osney bridge, dating from 1767, is the lone survivor. *Jackson's Oxford Journal* of 13 June 1767 carries an announcement of six large bridges to be erected in or near the city of Oxford the designs and proposals for which can be seen 'by applying to Mr Robert Taylor, in Spring Gardens'.

Though he worked for both Bishop Edmund Keene at Chester and Ely and Bishop Shute Barrington at Salisbury, remodelling the Bishops' palaces in all three places, Taylor only received three commissions for church work. A domed mausoleum was built to his designs in 1755 on the north side of Chilham Church in Kent,[15] for Robert Colebrooke (1718–84), who succeeded in 1752. According to Neale, it was a large circular building 42 feet in diameter, surmounted by a cupola. The chamber within was 24 feet in diameter, the 'sides divided into eight compartments, by Ionic columns, and containing receptacles for 42 bodies'. This plentiful provision can never have been put to full use for the mausoleum was demolished in 1862. Nor unfortunately did Malton engrave it, so its place in the long line of circular eighteenth-century mausoleums running from Hawksmoor's at Castle Howard (1729–36) to Wyatt's at Brockelsby (1787–94) is unknown. Both of these are circular and domed and it is tantalising not to know how Taylor's mausoleum related to them.

In 1776 Taylor designed a spire for St Peter's church in Wallingford (Plate 22), built a few years earlier in 1760–9.[16] On the square flint tower Taylor set an open Gothic octagonal base with the spire, in Pevsner's words, 'growing in a historically quite unauthorized curve out of it'. The spire is open work in all four stages. It is 'rather cheeky' for Sir Robert, 'but entirely convincing', Pevsner adds. The base was not as might be thought a bell-stage, for on 31 May 1776 Taylor wrote to the parish saying, 'I earnestly desire no bells be ever placed in the tower but if there be any it will be absolutely necessary to fix them in frames independent of the tower: which was not constructed for *both* bells and a spire in my opinion.'

Two years later Taylor provided alternative classical and gothic designs for a new church at Long Ditton in Surrey.[17] Both are on an identical Greek cross plan – the Gothic design has a spire exactly like that of St Peter's, Wallingford. The classical design (Plate 21), which was executed, is as usual astylar, with emphatic quoining, and lit by Diocletian windows – another neoclassical touch. The vestry minutes record Taylor's plans were approved on May 21, 1778; the builder was to be Edward Gray who worked for Taylor on many other commissions. What is impressive is the scale of the central domed tower. On a much smaller scale a similar motif was used on many of the Waterloo churches in the early nineteenth century. Though the design was relatively modest, Taylor was able to achieve maximum architectural impact, even persuading the parish to accept a Greek cross plan, always difficult in terms of Anglican liturgy. Not surprisingly, the arrangement ceased to appeal in the nineteenth century and the church was demolished in 1880.

Taylor's last public work was the Council House at Salisbury, executed with some alterations after his death by his pupil William Pilkington.[18] The foundation stone was laid on 14 October 1788, five days after Taylor's funeral. Malton's view (Plate 23) shows a handsome single-storey building with the Venetian windows set within relieving arches of which Taylor was so fond. Taylor here shows the same interest in modulating surfaces as was manifest in one of his first works, 35 Lincoln's Inn Fields – each arch is set within another arch, an anticipation of Soane's memorable design for the stables at the Royal Hospital, Chelsea. Other Taylor hallmarks are the canted bays, which he used here for the first time on a public building, and the forceful vermiculated rustication. Pilkington's alterations involved simplifying the windows and, more serious, filling in the central recession into which Taylor had set an elegant Tuscan colonnade. This spoilt the spirit of Taylor's design which is important for introducing in a medium-size public building a sense of movement, of advance and recession, such as he had developed from the outset of his career in his villas. Internally the plan was particularly interesting for its use of top-lighting (Plate 24). Here as in the Reduced Annuity Office at the Bank of England Taylor used a system of side-lit domes. Malton's engraving shows the Crown Court and the Nisi Prisus Court on the right flank of the building were to have circular domes resting on the walls and a cross-vaulted space at the sides. Here, however, the vaults no longer rest on columns but were simply to die into the walls – a step still closer to Soane.[19] Other interesting details are the concave entrance with steps inset, a detail suggestive of French neoclassicism. Subsequent alterations have eliminated much of the original character of the building. The recessed north portico was moved forward in 1829 by Thomas Hopper, and a first-floor room inserted above, while in 1889 the west portico was demolished and a projecting wing added. Extensive internal refitting was carried out in 1896–7.

It has been suggested that Taylor in his later years may have handed work to his pupils with the implication that they were responsible for some of the more interesting aspects of his last buildings. The fact that Pilkington's alterations reduced the originality and adventurousness of Taylor's designs suggests that this is not so. And as Taylor introduced side-lit domes at both Salisbury and the Bank it is likely he had a personal hand in both, especially as, at the Bank, it was Charles Beazley not Pilkington who was working under him.

A similar problem of master–pupil relationship arises over Admiralty House in Whitehall.[20] This is attributed in the *Survey of London* to Taylor's pupil S. P. Cockerell. Taylor, however, was responsible for the purchase of Sir Robert Barker's house which stood on the site on 15 September 1785 and on 16 December that year resold it for £3,200 to the Commissioners of the Navy. Walpole in his obituary describes Taylor as Surveyor to the Admiralty, and this is important as confirmation that he worked for the Navy as his name is not listed in the published lists of Admiralty and Navy Board office-holders.

The World on 17 April 1787 states categorically that the 'designs are Sir Robert Taylor's' but continues that 'after having compleated the designs, the estimate, (which, by the bye, is 14,000*l*) and all the other arrangements, Sir Robert generously relinquished the whole emoluments of the work to his assistant, Mr Cockerell – and resigned to him his Office of Surveyor to the Admiralty Board'.

Cockerell's name appears in the Admiralty records as directing the works, but this of course does not resolve the authorship of the original design. Externally the house has hallmarks of Taylor: it is astylar, of plain brick with stone dressings like other London houses. It is high-waisted with his characteristic string courses. The Venetian window in a relieving arch flanked by sash windows set in blind arches also echoes other late works. Within, various door-cases speak of Taylor – one in the dining room is flanked by half pilasters very similar to those on a doorway to the entrance hall in the Court Room suite at the Bank of England. Elsewhere the treatment is more complex (almost mannerist) than is usual with Taylor, notably the inner hall and the intriguing vaulting in the coves of the first-floor vestibule and reception room. The explanation may be that Taylor made the initial designs but that Cockerell introduced new elements in the interior. This would fit with the comment in *The World*, when ascribing the house to Taylor in 1787 that 'the walls are up, and it is covering in. The floors are not yet laid'.

If the precise role of Taylor remains unclear the origin of the commission can hardly be in doubt. For the First Lord of the Admiralty from December 1783 to July 1788 was none other than Admiral Lord Howe, for whom Taylor had built 3 Grafton Street and Porter's Lodge in Hertfordshire.

6 Great houses

Taylor designed two great houses, Gorhambury near St Albans, for the 3rd Viscount Grimston, and Heveningham (pronounced Heningham) in Suffolk for Sir Gerard Vanneck. Neither, alas, was completed to his original designs and this perhaps explains why Taylor's name is not better known as a result. At Gorhambury his original designs were set aside in favour of a less ambitious layout, and the interiors were for the most part executed in a very plain manner. At Heveningham Taylor was replaced by James Wyatt after the shell of the building was finished, and virtually the entire interior is Wyatt's.

Both commissions nonetheless have many points of interest, not least because both were for men with City backgrounds, whose wealth was relatively recent. James Bucknall's great-grandfather was Sir William Luckyn Bt of Little Waltham, Essex, whose wife Mary was the daughter of an alderman of London, William Sherrington. Sir William Luckyn's second son, William Grimston MP (*c.* 1683–1756), had succeeded in 1700 to Gorhambury and other large estates on the death of his great uncle Sir Samuel Grimston Bt and taken his name. William Grimston had again married a London girl, daughter of James Cooke, citizen of London, in 1706. In 1719 he was granted an Irish peerage as Viscount Grimston. The Gorhambury estates carried an important electoral interest in St Albans and after he himself was ousted from the seat in 1734 he continued to play a role behind the scenes, and Lord Egmont in his electoral survey of *c.* 1750 describes the Grimstons as 'totally belonging to the Duke of Newcastle' – a link with the group of Taylor patrons closely associated with the Duke. William's eldest son and heir, James Grimston, MP (1711–73), married in 1746 Mary, daughter of William Bucknall of Oxney Place in Watford – a neighbour of Thomas Villiers, 1st Earl of Clarendon, at the Grove Watford, who had commissioned Taylor to make alterations to his house about 1756. This James, the 2nd Viscount, was the father of James Bucknall Grimston MP (1747–1808), 3rd Viscount Grimston who brought in Taylor at Gorhambury.[1]

The history of Gorhambury has been told in some detail by J. C. Rogers.[2] Gorhambury, unlike many of Taylor's villas, was in every way an ancestral seat. It was the home of Francis Bacon. The old house was uninhabitable, according to Charlotte Grimston writing about 1819, 'the extreme want of repair rendered it quite unfit for habitation. All the best architects of the time were consulted as to the possibility of restoring it to a state of tolerable comfort, and security against cold and wet.' Unfortunately it is not known who 'all the best architects' were, but the exercise is of interest in itself as an example of serious consideration being given to preservation, presumably partly on grounds of associations with Bacon. In the end the Grimstons decided to do what Vanbrugh had recommended at Blenheim, to keep the old house as a ruin.

These discussions were taking place in 1775 when there is a bill from a Jos. Saunders, an otherwise unknown architect, for making working drawings of a summer house at Gorhambury (£10 10s), 'for surveying the House, giving instructions for shoring it, taking the plans of it' (£15 15s), and for 'making designs of a new house at Gorhambury, making fair drawings of ditto etc. (£52 10s)'. For some curious reason his account did not reach Lord Grimston until October 1789, who replied crustily: 'I must confess I was much astonished at the demand made up on me by your letter of yesterday, not having the smallest idea that a rough sketch, sent to me fifteen years ago could have been so valued.' With this aristocratic dismissal Mr Saunders returns to oblivion, to be replaced at the beginning of 1777 by Robert Taylor.

Thoughts for rebuilding the house were no doubt prompted by the 3rd Viscount Grimston's marriage in July 1774 to Henrietta, daughter of Edward Walter of Stalbridge Park, Dorset, and Bury Hill, near Dorking.

James Bucknall Grimston (1747–1808) had succeeded his father as 3rd Viscount a year before his marriage: as this was an Irish peerage he was able to stand as an MP on two occasions in 1783 and 1784, only retiring when in 1790 he was granted an

English peerage as Baron Verulam. Lord Grimston had been on the grand tour and his father-in-law was a considerable collector whose pictures passed to his daughter.

A major feature of Taylor's first plans (Plate 3) was a large picture gallery, and also an apartment for Mr Walter on the main floor consisting of bed and dressing room where the old man could be near his pictures.

Taylor's first design is interesting as it shows the villa plan being applied to a great house. Sir John Summerson in his Royal Society of Arts lectures[3] traces the decline of the great house and the ascendancy of the villa – and their fusion half-way in such houses as Kedleston which were at once great houses and villas. Taylor's first scheme for Gorhambury has the dominant central hall of the early Palladian villas, apparently on a Pantheon plan quite close to his rotunda at the Bank of England. Unusually, the main entrance opens direct into a combined hall and staircase, divided by a screen of columns – the central arch presumably being elliptical. The staircase itself was an oval one, of one flight dividing into two. This is the only instance of Taylor using this form, except possibly at 3 Grafton Street. Apart from Mr Walter's quite modest little apartment there was to be no state apartment on the main floor but a suite of rooms beginning with Lord Grimston's octagonal dressing room leading directly from the hall – presumably a business room. This led in sequence into a library, drawing room, picture gallery and eating room. In addition there were three apsed vestibules, four secondary or back staircases, and a water-closet, just off the entrance hall, an eighteenth-century anticipation of the downstairs 'gents' cloakroom'.

Externally the main front had a 2–3–2 window rhythm (Plate 2) rather than the villa's usual 1–3–1, but this was still compact in terms of the accommodation within. Though the house was to be entirely faced in ashlar, Taylor's treatment was to be as austere as his villas, no architraves to the windows, a simple cornice running round the house, in contrast to the full entablature on the portico, and only a low parapet of coping stones – as in early villas like Barlaston.

This was Taylor's ideal treatment. His revised designs are considerably more conventional. The house now has a full entablature on all fronts with a continuous balustrade above (Plate 4), and the main front has a 3–3–3 bay rhythm very much like the standard run of larger Palladian seats in the mid-eighteenth-century.

Internally the house now has a large two-storey hall – looking back to the baroque entrance halls of great houses at the beginning of the century, and here clearly modelled on Inigo Jones's cube hall in the Queen's House at Greenwich. The staircase has become somewhat smaller but is still characteristically oval in shape and top-lit. The picture gallery has been replaced by a saloon, but a small apartment of bed and dressing room, perhaps still for Mr Walter, is incorporated; and the rooms unusually have cross-vaulted ceilings, an echo of Taylor's later work elsewhere and an anticipation of a favourite motif of Sir John Soane.

On 20 October 1784 Lord Grimston recorded that he 'took possession of our new house at G on this day, after having been employed in building it seven years the second of last month'. Huge quantities of bricks were used – only the outer facing being of stone. Clay was dug and brick burned on the estate by Mr Bodimead. Between 1777 and 1782, fifty kilns yielded 1,564,800 bricks, which at 17s per 1,000, and lime burnt at 12s per hundredweight, cost £2,149 18s 7½d. Wood for burning the bricks cost £369 9s 3d. The actual bricklaying during the same period by Thomas White and Thomas Chambers cost £764 3s 3d. The master masons were John Wildsmith, Joseph Hawke, and a Mr Westmacott, and the total charged for stone and stonework was £5,505 4s 11½d. Lead was supplied by John Kent of St Albans, and he carried out the plumbing. His total bill was £1,039 3s 9¼d. The Coade stone capitals of the portico supplied by Mrs Coade cost £342 3s. In total the main block cost £16,862 3s 6d.

For reasons that are not quite clear Taylor's final bill was not presented until after his death, when his son Michelangelo Taylor charged £938 19s, made up of £843 2s commission at 5 per cent, £63 for journeys and £32 17s for models. Before the account was settled there was some dispute over Taylor's charges, with Lord Grimston observing that 'Taylor measured no part of the work and settled none of the bills with workmen' and that 'although Mr Taylor has charged in his account 20 visits to Gorhambury seven is the most that Sir Robert made from the commencement of the visit to the last hour'. Taylor, it seems, provided plans but supervision was carried out by his clerks. On October 16, 1777 he replied to a query from Lord Grimston about the provision of scaffolding: '... upon looking into the agreement with the mason ... (Mr Taylor) finds they are as well as the bricklayer, to provide all manner of scaffolding. Mr Taylor will certainly send his clerk by one of the coaches on Tuesday (no coach going out on Monday) to examine and measure the work.'

The wings, though shown on Malton's plans, were not begun until just before Taylor's death. Shortly after his funeral there is a letter from Taylor's former pupil, William Pilkington, soliciting the post of surveyor to Lord Grimston. Though Malton shows one of them as a kitchen block there must initially have been kitchens in the basement of the main block. Accounts show that they were built between 1788 and 1792 and cost £3,218 8s 6d. They were not sited as Taylor intended in front of the house in the usual Palladian manner and linked by quadrant corridors, but instead were directly in line with the house.

As a result, two of the main rooms – the dining room and drawing room – looked down over the kitchens, which greatly annoyed Lady Verulam, who set herself on pulling the south wing down. In 1817 a new building was added between the main block and north wing, upsetting the symmetry of the plan to a distressing extent, but perhaps less disturbing in the age of the picturesque when marked irregularity was acceptable even in classical buildings. Thomas Martin, the contractor, submitted a bill for £3,547 16s 6d. In 1826 further remodelling took place under the architect William Atkinson – the south wing was demolished and the north wing enlarged and on 14 March that year Lord Verulam noted in his diary that 'the wing being nearly down, opens a pleasing view of Pre Wood and I think improves very materially the appearance of the house, which I trust will be made infinitely better by this measure of Lady Verulam's'.

The plasterwork at Gorhambury was carried out by John Rose, whose total bill came to £985 15s 8d. This was presumably the same John Rose who worked for Taylor at the Bank of England and is another instance of Taylor using the same

builders and craftsmen on different commissions. Architecturally one of the most interesting aspects of Gorhambury is the
treatment of the corridors showing Taylor experimenting again
with top lighting. On the first floor there is a broad cross vaulted
corridor with top lights inset in alternate sections. These
however only borrow light from another corridor above which is
also top lit with lights in the top of semi circular domes.

Taylor's other great country house is Heveningham near
Yoxford in Suffolk. The first sight of Heveningham from the
passing public road is one of the most spectacular of any country
house in England. Here in remote, sparsely populated countryside a majestic front over 200 feet long comes suddenly in view,
seen to perfect advantage on rising ground across a lake against a
backcloth of magnificent park trees. At Heveningham there was
originally no ha-ha. The parkland laps against the walls of the
house and it remains a perfect expression of the age of Capability
Brown – a great classical house in an idealised natural setting
with gardens, terraces, walks and shrubberies all banished out of
sight at the back. With its columned centrepiece and pedimented
end pavilions Heveningham has the air of a terrace of houses
overlooking a square in London or Bath, and this feeling is
heightened by the use of a continuous arcade at ground-floor
level – just the kind of arcade architects used to bring discipline
to the alternating rhythm of doors and windows on such
terraces.

What is striking about Taylor's composition is its bold model-
ling. The centrepiece (Plate 6) has a free-standing colonnade with
paired columns or pilasters. On the end pavilions the engaged
columns are again virtually in the round, here coupled with
pilasters that turn the corners. The vertical articulation is equally
emphatic: the entablatures of the centrepiece and end pavilions
oversail the cornice and balustrade of the intervening ranges.
This was a device used later by William Wilkins to good effect at
St George's Hospital on Hyde Park Corner. At ground-floor level
rustication is restricted to the centre and the ends, again making
them stand out from the rest of the front.

The composition is given added *gravitas* by the massive attic
above the central colonnade – on the scale of the attic of a Roman
triumphal arch. Taylor must have had such models in mind as the

three central bays are adorned with statues of the four seasons set against the attic. Above these, reclining female figures, one with an overflowing cornucopia, the other with a spear, act as supporters to a shield with the Vanneck coat of arms.

This use of powerful central attic suggests the possibility of influence from the Parisian mint, La Monnaie, on the Seine, built to the designs of Jacques-Denis Antoine in 1768–75, where again it is used as the centrepiece of a very long front, though La Monnaie is without the end pavilions.

From a distance Heveningham appears to be of stone (Plate 5), but in fact it is all stucco and it is this that brings to mind Nash's terraces in Regent's Park. Nash of course was Taylor's pupil and it does not seem wholly fanciful to see in Nash's endless variations of the palace-terrace theme the true progeny of Taylor's Heveningham.

Sir Joshua Vanneck had acquired the Heveningham estate in 1752, perhaps with an eye to obtaining a parliamentary seat. Twelve years later he obtained control of one seat at Dunwich, a rotten borough, famous or infamous because it was supposedly on electorate without voters, having fallen into the sea, (though in fact there were some thirty or forty voters). Sir Joshua's son Gerard was returned for Dunwich in 1768 and sat continuously until 1790.

When Sir Joshua died in 1777 he was described in the *Gentleman's Magazine* as 'one of the richest merchants in Europe'. Suckling's *Antiquities of Suffolk* (1848) implies Sir Gerard began Heveningham as soon as he inherited. The same year he also embarked on the remodelling of Roehampton Grove in Surrey, which he had recently acquired. At Roehampton his architect was James Wyatt and this may help explain why at Heveningham he broke with Taylor and entrusted the interior decoration to James Wyatt.

Unfortunately all the estate papers have disappeared, possibly in a fire in the estate office in the 1950s, so there is virtually no documentation. However, the house appears to have been largely complete by 1784, when it is described in some detail by François de la Rochefoucauld. 'In earlier times', he wrote, there was a small and very old house which had sunk to a very low condition indeed, though its site was a pleasant one ... Sir

Gerard had all the partitions pulled down and constructed a hall or vestibule out of the old house. All the rest has been added.' Some details of the earlier house are given in a letter from Sir Joshua Vanneck to Dr Ducarel dated 19 September 1754: '. . . the old house built by the family who gave their name to this village, has been pulled down about forty years ago; the present house being built at that time by one Squire Bence.'

Taylor's original plan for the house was engraved by Malton, and when this is compared with the plan of the house today it is clear that Wyatt was working within Taylor's shell, changing the uses and decoration of the rooms but not their overall proportions. Malton also provides a view of the hall as Taylor intended. This shows a two-storey atrium with an Ionic order below and a Corinthian one above. Though Malton suggests by the scale of his figures that the ground floor was very lofty, the columns would in fact have been quite short (as in other Taylor houses), rising only just above the level of the windows. Wyatt's hall is on an altogether grander scale: to achieve this he blocked out all the first-floor windows in the centre of the main front (which would have lit Taylor's gallery). This was a bold stroke indeed, and one which produced one of the noblest neoclassical rooms in the country.

In recent years the future of Heveningham, like that of some of Taylor's villas, has been the cause of major concern. The house and parkland were placed in a discretionary trust in the 1950s which under subsequent legislation became liable to capital gains tax every fifteen years. The owners threatened to break up the house unless the government acquired it and in 1970 Heveningham and 400 acres was acquired for £303,662, paid for out of the Land Fund. It had been hoped that the house would be transferred to the National Trust but the government was unwilling to provide an endowment and in 1981 Heveningham was sold to a private buyer, who has undertaken to continue opening it to the public. The proceeds, £706,780, were paid into the new National Heritage Memorial Fund.

Conclusion

Do Taylor's works entitle him to a 'distinguished place in the first rank of British architects' as his memorial tablet in Poets' Corner proclaims? Today we would probably restrict the first rank to pioneers and household names such as Smythson, Inigo Jones, Wren, Vanbrugh, Hawksmoor, Adam, Soane, Nash, Burges, Mackintosh and Lutyens. Amidst such a pantheon there might be arguments as to whether Hugh May or Sir Roger Pratt would qualify , or even Gibbs, Chambers and Barry. But seen from the perspective of 1788 the assessment is much more reasoned – the very term 'architect' had only come into widespread use in the eighteenth century and Taylor's additions to the Bank of England alone would have earned him a position high among his contemporaries. At a time when architects were seeking to establish themselves as a profession Taylor had been a remarkably successful exponent of professionalism. He was a model of industry and competence and had handled a vast volume of work through a well organised office. He was one of the first architects to take on pupils in the modern sense, and showed great concern over their training and future careers. According to Walpole, Taylor on his deathbed 'suspended the consolations of religion, literally full half an hour, till he had finished various letters in favour of Mr Cockerell and Mr Craig the architects, who had been his pupils, to get them new patronage, to secure them better in what they had got!'[1]

In terms of English Palladianism Taylor unquestionably belongs to the second generation – beginning work some thirty years after Burlington, Campbell and Kent. However his domestic architecture, his villas and town houses do earn him Walpole's judgement that he was possessed of those 'independent, original powers, which are reciprocally self-formed and self-forming'.[2]

His astylar elevations, on almost all his domestic buildings, take Palladianism a long way down the road to neoclassicism, towards an architecture of simple geometric volumes, plain surfaces and ingeniously varied plans. In this he shows a boldness beyond any of his contemporaries – he was prepared and able to make strong architectural statements, dispensing with virtually all external enrichments and dressings. This boldness is particularly apparent in the siting of his villas – he had a very sure and confident eye in placing all his buildings so they would be seen to best effect, and in turn command spectacular views over the countryside around. This is evident at once at Harleyford, in many ways quite a small and plain house, but set so strikingly close to the Thames that it dominates a whole stretch of the river and holds the attention of anyone passing by boat as each of the three fronts visable from the water is treated quite differently.

The same boldness is evident in his plans. Taylor broke from the traditional grouping of rooms into apartments – consisting of ante-room, bedroom, cabinet and closet – and instead provided his patrons with large living rooms on the main floor, in the villas a saloon, dining room and library, setting all the bedrooms on the upper floor. In this way he anticipated a fundamental change in planning. His rotunda at the Bank of England is one of the first of the modern covered exchanges, just as his Transfer Offices with the clerks and counters ranged around the walls anticipate the typical nineteenth- and twentieth-century banking hall.

Though his style has strong personal hallmarks throughout his career it shows a steady evolution from one decade to another; in the 1750s there are strong rococo elements and a tendency towards elaboration and complexity, in the 1760s a greater simplicity in both plans and decoration. The 1770s sees a further move towards neoclassicism with the atrium at Purbrook, and the opening up of one space into another as at both Purbrook and Sharpham. In the early 1780s there is something of a gap in the list of works, perhaps to be associated with his term as Sheriff of the City and his knighthood. However, in the three or four years before his death there is suddenly a new burst of originality with the side-lit domes of the Reduced Annuity Office at the Bank and at the Guildhall.

With these late works there must be some question how far they may have been in the hands of pupils. Yet if this was the case it would seem likely that the most original developments would be associated with particular pupils – when in fact at the Bank it was Beazley working under Taylor, while at the Guildhall at Salisbury it was Pilkington who executed Taylor's designs after his death. Neither of these men, though competent practitioners, produced work of such originality in later life. Taylor's side-lit dome was of course to be developed with brilliant effect by Soane, his successor at the Bank. It is an interesting parting thought to wonder how much Taylor's most famous pupil, Nash, may have taken from Taylor, consciously or unconsciously, even though his remarks about Taylor 'making shift to get on' hardly suggest admiration. Yet Nash's use of broken plans, of projecting bays and bows, of octagons, ellipses and circles all echo Taylor as do his light, elegant, stone cantilevered staircases. And in the Royal Mews there is a curious and unexpected play on Taylor's hanging domes in the Bank Transfer Offices. In the two ranges of stables at the back of the Mews quadrangle (one of which now houses a collection of Royal coaches) there are colonnades on either side behind which are the stalls for the horses. At a glance the aisles look as if they carry a series of shallow domes – the motif Taylor borrowed from Gibbs' St Martin-in-the-Fields. In fact the 'domes' are flat – but the illusion works and the unconscious tribute to Taylor is remarkable.

Chronological list of works

Note: see also the list in Howard Colvin's *Dictionary of British Architects 1600–1840* (1978), where Taylor's works are classified by building types. For the appropriate documentation see the discussions of buildings in the text and footnotes.

14 ST JAMES'S SQUARE, LONDON. Alterations in 1748–50 for Peter Du Cane. Sir Charles Asgill occupied the house 1768–73; it was rebuilt in 1896–98 for the London Library.

112 BISHOPSGATE STREET, CITY OF LONDON. For John Gore *c*. 1750. Demolished.

BRAXTED LODGE, ESSEX. Altered and enlarged for Peter Du Cane 1752–6.

THE BISHOP'S PALACE, CHESTER. Remodelled for Edmund Keene, Bishop of Chester (and later Bishop of Ely) 1754–7. Demolished 1874.

35 and 36 LINCOLN'S INN FIELDS, LONDON. For Sir Thomas Sewell and Sir (Anthony) Thomas Abdy Bt, 1754–7. No. 35 destroyed 1941. No. 36 rebuilt 1859.

MAUSOLEUM AT CHILHAM CHURCH, KENT. For Robert Colebrooke. Faculty granted 24 October 1754. Demolished 1862.

HARLEYFORD MANOR, NEAR GREAT MARLOW, BUCK-INGHAMSHIRE. For Sir William Clayton, Bt. Under construction in 1755. (Being restored and adapted as offices in 1983).

COPTFOLD HALL, NEAR MARGERETTING, ESSEX. Built for Richard Holden soon after he acquired the estate in November 1755. Demolished 1850.

LONDON BRIDGE, with George Dance senior, removal of houses on bridge, replacement of two central arches by a single arch, and erection of balustrades, 1756–66. Demolished 1831.

BARLASTON HALL, NEAR STONE, STAFFORDSHIRE (*Attributed*). For Thomas Mills, under construction in 1756–7. (Restoration by Save Britain's Heritage began October 1981).

THE GROVE, WATFORD, HERTFORDSHIRE. Alterations for Thomas Villiers, 1st Earl of Clarendon, *c*. 1756.

70 LOMBARD STREET, CITY OF LONDON. Banking house for Sir Charles Asgill, Bt *c*. 1756. Demolished *c*. 1920.

GRAFTON HOUSE, PICCADILLY, LONDON. For the 3rd Duke of Grafton, *c.* 1760; afterwards remodelled for the Turf Club, 1876. Demolished 1966.

LONGFORD CASTLE, NEAR SALISBURY, WILTSHIRE. Additions for 1st Viscount Folkstone, *c.* 1760.

OTTERSHAW PARK, NEAR CHERTSEY, SURREY. Built for Sir Thomas Sewell soon after he acquired the property in April 1761. Demolished 1908.

ASGILL HOUSE, RICHMOND, SURREY. For Sir Charles Asgill, Bt 1761–4. (Restored by Mr Fred Hauptführer and now vested in the Palladian Trust).

DANSON HILL, BEXLEYHEATH, KENT. For Sir John Boyd, 1762–7. (owned by the London Borough of Bexley, still awaiting restoration in 1983).

TREWITHEN, NEAR TRURO, CORNWALL. Dining room and other alterations for Thomas Hawkins, *c.* 1763–4. (Open to the public).

BANK BUILDINGS, CITY OF LONDON. Two blocks of offices on Threadneedle Street opposite the Bank of England, 1764–6. Demolished 1844.

THE BANK OF ENGLAND, CITY OF LONDON. Rotunda and transfer offices to the east of Sampson's original building, 1765–8; Court Room and associated offices, 1765–72; extensions to the west of Sampson's building including Reduced Annuity Office, 1787. Some of Taylor's work was rebuilt by his successor Sir John Soane; the rest disappeared during remodelling by Sir Herbert Baker in 1921–37. Taylor's Court Room, however, was reconstructed on an upper floor of Baker's new building, but the detail simplified and altered.

ARNO'S GROVE, SOUTHGATE, MIDDLESEX. Library and dining room for Sir George Colebrooke, Bt probably *c.* 1765.

34 SPRING GARDENS, CHARING CROSS, LONDON. For himself before 1767. Demolished 1885.

KEVINGTON, ST MARY CRAY, KENT. Enlarged for Herman Behrens 1767–9.

OXFORD. Six minor bridges on the Botley Road of which Osney Bridge is a survivor. 1767.

SWINFORD BRIDGE, EYNSHAM (*Attributed*). For the 4th Earl of Abingdon, 1767–9.

33 UPPER BROOK STREET, MAYFAIR, LONDON. For Sir John Boyd, 1767–8; Sir Henry Houghton Bt moved in in 1769.

1–14 GRAFTON STREET, MAYFAIR, LONDON. For the 3rd Duke of Grafton 1768 onwards. Only Nos 3–6 survive and the basement and staircase at No. 7. The first residents in the houses were as follows (the dates are those of the first entry entered in the rate books):

1 Sir George Warren (1775 at £210 rent)
2 Mr William Gale (1776 at £90)
3 Admiral Lord Howe (1771 at £240; then £210)
4 Lord Villiers (1771 at £100; 1775 onwards at £210)
5 Arnold Nesbitt (1772 at £160)
6 Robert Thornton (1792 at £130)
7 Sir John Boyd (1773 at £130)
8 Sir Ralph Payne (1786 at £130, possibly occupied earlier)
9 ?
10 Lord Molesworth (1775 at £80, preceded for one year only by Robert Piggot, Esq.)
11 ? Crawford (1772 at £100)
12 Hon. Mrs Caroline Howe (1771 at £70)
13 Mrs Baddesley (1772 at £70)
14 John Stewart (1771 at £40, from 1773, Mrs Stewart)

CHUTE LODGE, NEAR ANDOVER, WILTSHIRE. For John Freeman. Under construction *c.* 1768; later enlarged. Recently divided, with the adjoining wings, into four houses.

PURBROOK HOUSE, PORTSDOWN HILL, HAMPSHIRE. For Peter Taylor, *c.* 1770. Demolished 1829.

SHARPHAM HOUSE, NEAR TOTNES, DEVON. For Captain Philemon Pownoll, *c.* 1770.

THE OAKS, CARSHALTON, SURREY (*Attributed*). Dining room or ball-room for General John Burgoyne, *c.* 1770. Demolished.

BISHOP'S PALACE, ELY, CAMBRIDGESHIRE. Alterations for Bishop Edmund Keene on his appointment to the see in 1771. Little of Taylor's work is identifiable today.

ALTHORP, NORTHAMPTONSHIRE. Repairs for the 1st Earl Spencer after part of the roof collapsed in 1772.

THORNCROFT, LEATHERHEAD, SURREY. For Henry Crabb Boulton, 1772.

SPENCER HOUSE, ST JAMES'S PLACE, LONDON. Decoration of the ceiling of the staircase for the 1st Earl Spencer, 1772.

MAIDENHEAD BRIDGE, BERKSHIRE. 1772–7.

ELY HOUSE, 37 DOVER STREET, MAYFAIR, LONDON. For Edmund Keene, Bishop of Ely 1772–6; interior remodelled 1909. Now the London home of the Oxford University Press.

PORTER'S LODGE, SHENLEY, HERTFORDSHIRE. For Admiral Lord Howe soon after 1772; altered 1903; now part of mental hospital.

STONE BUILDINGS, LINCOLN'S INN, LONDON. 1774–80. South pavilion completed by P. Hardwick, 1842–5. Taylor's original scheme was for a building of nearly double the length.

THE SIX CLERKS' AND ENROLMENT OFFICES, CHANCERY LANE, LONDON. For Lincoln's Inn. 1775–77.

THE ASSEMBLY ROOM ABOVE THE OLD EXCHANGE, BELFAST, IRELAND. 1776, exterior altered 1845 by C. Lanyon; interior by W.H. Lynn in 1895.

ST PETER'S CHURCH, WALLINGFORD, BERKSHIRE. The Gothic spire 1776–77.

HEVENINGHAM HALL, NEAR YOXFORD, SUFFOLK. For Sir Gerard Vanneck 1777–c.1780; interior almost all by James Wyatt, c. 1780–4. Open to the public.

GORHAMBURY, NEAR ST ALBANS, HERTFORDSHIRE. For the 3rd Viscount Grimston 1777–90, alterations by W. Atkinson in 1816–17 and 1826–28 and W. Burn 1847. Open to the public.

LONG DITTON CHURCH, SURREY. Contract dated 1778. Demolished 1880.

BISHOP'S PALACE, SALISBURY, WILTSHIRE. Alterations including Gothic porch, doors, windows and chimneypiece for Bishop Shute Barrington, soon after 1782.

ADMIRALTY HOUSE, WHITEHALL, LONDON. Built 1786–88 as the official residence of the First Lord of the Admiralty (who between 1783 and 1788 was Admiral Lord Howe). The interior is largely by S. P. Cockerell but the exterior and basic plan may be Taylor's.

THE GUILDHALL, SALISBURY, WILTSHIRE. Executed, with some alterations, to Taylor's designs in 1788–95, by his pupil W. Pilkington. Later altered.

WHITEHALL YARD, LONDON. Taylor designed a house for his son, Michelangelo, on this site in 1788 but it does not appear to have been begun until 1793. Taylor's design was probably modified in execution, perhaps by one of his pupils.

Undated 15 PHILPOT LANE, LONDON.

Undated CLUMBER PARK, NOTTINGHAMSHIRE. Work including a room with a screen of columns at either end for the Duke of Newcastle.

Notes

Introduction

1 *The Farington Diary*, ed. J. Grieg 5 November 1811. viii, p. 300.
2 David Watkin, *The Life and Work of C. R. Cockerell*, 1974, p. 61.
3 *The Farington Diary*, 27 August 1807. iv, 192.
4 Horace Walpole, *Anecdotes of Painting*, ed. Hilles and Daghlian, V, 1937, p. 192.
5 *Gentleman's Magazine*, 1820, ii, p. 38.
6 John Summerson, Fourth edition, 1963, p. 219.
7 *The Penguin Dictionary of Architecture* ed. J. Fleming, Hugh Honour and Nikolaus Pevsner, 1964, p. 221.
8 H. R. Steele and F. R. Yerbury, *The Old Bank of England*, 1930, p. 7.
9 New edition in the Classical America Series on Art and Architecture, 1982, p. 14.
10 Pan Books edition, 1960, p. 223.
11 Thomas Hardwick, 'Memoir of the Life of Sir William Chambers', prefixed to Gwilt's edition of Chambers's *Treatise on Civic Architecture*, 1825, p. xlix.
12 *The London Chronicle*, September 27–30, 1788, p. 319.
13 See *Books from the Library of Sir Robert Taylor in the Library at the Taylor Institution, Oxford*, a checklist compiled by D. J. Gilson, 1973.
14 A set of Malton's plates survives at the Ashmolean Museum, Oxford, with some of Malton's original drawings. There is another set at Sir John Soane's Museum. (? and the Cortauld?).
15 *The World* is available on microfilm in the British Library, Burney Collection.
16 See John Fleming, *Robert Adam and his Circle*, 1962, pp. 315–17.
17 Quoted in David Watkin, op. cit., p. 61.

1 Life

1 Walpole, *Anecdotes*, V, p. 192.
2 Walpole, *Anecdotes*, V, p. 192.
3 Gunnis, *Dictionary*, p. 381.
4 Walpole, *Anecdotes*, V, p. 193.
5 Inland Revenue Books at the Public Record Office, Book 13, folio 119.
6 The Court Books of the Masons' Company at the Guildhall Library record that the elder Taylor last appeared at a committee meeting on 30 September, 1742. On 14 October in a list of members of the company he is entered as dead.

7 Walpole, *Anecdotes*, V. p. 193.
8 Walpole Society, *Vertue Notebooks*, III, 161 entry for June 1752.
9 Walpole, *Anecdotes*, V, p. 193.
10 Gunnis, *Dictionary*, p. 251.
11 Walpole, *Anecdotes*, V, p. 193.
12 Commissioned by Act of Parliament in 1747.
13 Gunnis, *Dictionary*, p. 382.
14 Court Books of the Masons' Company at the Guildhall Library, London.
15 Walpole, *Anecdotes*, V, p. 193.
16 Walpole, *Anecdotes*, V, p. 193.
17 *Survey of London*, XXIX, 141.
18 Essex Record Office D/DDC A18; and Nancy Briggs in *Essex Journal*, V, 1970, pp. 97–102.
19 Walpole, *Anecdotes*, V, p. 195.
20 Walpole, *Anecdotes*, V, p. 198.
21 Walpole, *Anecdotes*, V, p. 195.
22 *London Chronicle*, 1788 LXIV, p. 319.
23 Walpole, *Anecdotes*, V, p. 194.
24 Colvin, *Dictionary*, pp. 982–3.
25 Public Record Office, Office of Works *Minutes, Proceedings*, vols 14–16.
26 APSD states Taylor 'commenced Coldbath Fields house of correction, continued by Sir William Chambers and T. Rogers'.
27 Walpole, *Anecdotes*, V, p. 196.
28 Walpole, *Anecdotes*, V, pp. 196–7.
29 Walpole, *Anecdotes*, V, p. 197.
30 *The Times*, 10 and 11 October 1788.

2 Patronage

1 Namier and Brooke, *House of Commons*, III, p. 574.
2 *The Builder*, 24 October 1846.
3 David Watkin, *C. R. Cockerell*, 1974, p. 61.
4 *Bulletin of the Institute of Historical Research*, 44, pp. 68–75.
5 Namier and Brooke, *House of Commons*, III, pp. 586–7.
6 Namier and Brooke, *House of Commons*, III, pp. 587–8.
7 Namier and Brooke, *House of Commons*, III, pp. 607–9.
8 Walpole, *Anecdotes*, V, p. 193.
9 *Gentleman's Magazine*, 1788, II, p. 1070.
10 A faculty was granted in 1771.
11 Romney Sedgwick, *House of Commons*, II, pp. 65–6. Dates given for directorships omit short statutory intervals.
12 *Survey of London*, III, p. 43.
13 Romney Sedgwick, *House of Commons*, II, p. 123.
14 Minutes of the Court of Governors, 31 December 1746.
15 Romney Sedgwick, *House of Commons*, II, pp. 70–1.
16 *Gentleman's Magazine*, 1788, II, p. 1070.
17 *DNB; Gentleman's Magazine*, 1788, II, p. 840.

18 *Survey of London*, XXIX, p. 141.

19 Namier and Brooke, *House of Commons*, II, pp. 235–7.

20 Namier and Brooke, *House of Commons*, II, p. 237.

21 *Thraliana: The Diary of Mrs Hester Lynch Thrale 1776–1809*, 1942, p. 334.

22 Namier and Brooke, *House of Commons*, III, pp. 194–5.

23 *Thraliana*, 1942, p. 804.

24 Namier and Brooke, *House of Commons*, III, pp. 195–6.

25 Among the Grafton Papers in the Suffolk Record Office is a letter of 26 June 1781 (ref. Acc 423/419) from Jos. Sharpe to the Duke of Grafton concerning a house in Grafton Street built by Mr Fordyce, who is described as bankrupt. *Thraliana*, 1942, p. 335.

26 Nancy Briggs in *Essex Journal*, V, 1970, pp. 97–102.

27 Romney Sedgwick, *House of Commons*, II, p. 117.

28 Namier and Brooke, *House of Commons*, III, p. 525.

29 Namier and Brooke, *House of Commons*, II, pp. 267–8.

30 Namier and Brooke *House of Commons*, III, p. 456.

31 *Complete Baronetage*.

32 *DNB; Complete Peerage*; Namier and Brooke, III, pp. 253–4.

33 *Complete Baronetage*. For details of Sir John's life I am grateful to one of his descendants, Mrs Diana Phillips.

34 Information from the Catalogue of Freeman Family Papers in the Gloucestershire Record Office.

35 *DNB*.

36 Namier and Brooke, *House of Commons*, II, p. 106.

37 Namier and Brooke, *House of Commons*, III, pp. 302–3.

38 Sir Lewis Namier, *Structure of Politics at the Accession of George III*, 1963, pp. 50–1.

39 ibid. p. 55.

40 C. and A. Nesbitt, *History of the Family of Nisbet or Nesbitt*, 1898, 58.

41 Namier and Brooke, *House of Commons*, III, pp. 517–18.

42 Walpole, *Anecdotes*, V, p. 198; Namier and Brooke, *House of Commons*, II, pp. 319–20.

43 Namier, *Structure of Politics*, p. 218.

44 ibid. p. 218.

45 Namier and Brooke, *House of Commons*, III, pp. 422–3.

46 Namier and Brooke, *House of Commons*, II, pp. 1–2.

47 M. W. Greenslade *Barlaston: a history*, published by Keele University, 1966. *Aris's Birmingham Gazette*, 31 May 1742.

48 *Country Life*, 17 and 24 April 1969.

49 *DNB; Complete Peerage*; Namier and Brooke, *House of Commons*, II, p. 649.

50 Namier and Brooke, *House of Commons*, II, pp. 141–5.

51 David Watkin, *C. R. Cockerell*, 1974, p. 61.

52 She had married a Mr John Howe – Sir Nathanial Wraxall, *Memoirs*, V, p. 35.

53 Information kindly supplied by the late Lord Spencer from the archives at Althorp. For Taylor's work at Spencer House see *Survey of London*, XXX, 521 and pl. 257a.

54 Thomas Hardwick, 'Memoir of the Life of Sir William Chambers', prefixed to Gwilt's edition of Chambers's *Treatise on Civil Architecture*, 1825, p. xlix.

3   Villas

1 Walpole, *Visits to Country Seats*, Walpole Society, xvi.

2 Charles Middleton, *Picturesque and Architectural Views for Cottages, Farm Houses, and Country Villas*, 1793, p. 3.

3 'The old manor-house of Harleyford ... was pulled down in 1755, when a handsome regular mansion was erected on the same spot ... from a design of Sir Robert Taylor's' (pp. 99–100).

4 Namier and Brooke, *House of Commons*, II, pp. 219–20.

5 Buckinghamshire Record Office, Clayton Family Papers, Marlow Book, 1747–57. Information kindly supplied by E. J. Davis, County Architect.

6 Sir William Clayton married, first, in 1745, Mary, daughter of John Warde of Squerryes. There is also an engraving after the painting.

7 Mrs Lybbe Powis, *Diaries*. Mrs Powis adds that Mr Clayton's elegant brick house was after the model of Lord Harcourt's. Though the house Stiff Leadbetter built at Nuneham Courtenay was indeed of brick (it was later encased in stone by Capability Brown) it was not begun until 1756, a little later than Harleyford.

8 The domed corridor to the right is a puzzle. During restoration in 1982 it was apparent that the brickwork on the entrance front side had been crudely hacked out to make space for the niches but it is not clear if this change took place soon after the house was built or in the 19th century.

9 *Country Life*, 4 June 1910, page 810.

10 Essex Record Office: Deeds, D/DBT 811; 1828 sale D/DO p. B7, B123/737–45. See also W. White *Directory of Essex*, 1848: D. W. Coller *People's History of Essex*, p. 125–6.

11 Romney Sedgwick, *House of Commons*, II, pp. 144–5.

12 M. W. Greenslade, *Barlaston: a history*, published by Keele University, 1966 and 1974. See also *Aris's Birmingham Gazette*, 31 May 1742; J. Sleigh, *History of Leek*, 1862; and *Country Life*, 18 April 1968, where Andor Gomme first attributed the house to Taylor.

13 Greenslade, *Barlaston*, p. 22.

14 This was first noted by John Greenacombe of the *Survey of London*.

15 At Danson there is evidence that it may originally have been intended to set the roof behind a parapet. The external structural walls (of brick) are carried up within the roof for about 2 feet and holes were cut through for the main joists of the roof. See Roger White, *Danson Hill Archaeologia Cantiana*, 1983.

16 See Roger White, ibid., and Ruth Hutcheson, *The History of Danson*, published by the author, 1979.

17 Frederick Hauptführer, *Guide to Asgill House*; Christopher Hussey in *Country Life*, 9 June 1944, p. 992.

18 Information from Mrs Joan Longridge. There is also a sermon by Joseph Kelsey, rector of Newton-Tony in Wiltshire (printed in 1673) preached 'at the consecration of a chappel in the House of John Collins, Esq. of Chute'.

19 Ann Finer and George Savage (eds), *The Selected Letters of Josiah Wedgwood*, 1965, p. 114.

20 Among the Freeman Papers in the Gloucestershire Record Office.

21 *Salisbury and Winchester Journal*, 14 September 1795, information from Mrs Barbara Hasler.

22 The catalogue of architectural drawings sold at Christie's on 30 Nov. 1983 (lot 182) includes a drawing for the ceiling of the dining room at Chute. Lot 184 is inscribed 'if this should not please then Mr Taylor desires Mr Freeman will please to write'.

23 White's *Directory for Hampshire* (1878) states that the house was demolished in 1829 by John Walker and in 1840 replaced by a new house in the Grecian architecture by John Deverell.

24 See also the author in *Country Life*, 17 and 24 April 1969, and Oxley Durent Parker, *Sharpham*, a paper, afterwards printed, read to the Antiquarian Association of Totnes, 18 January 1921.

25 The wall between the two ovals has been largely removed but Parker *Sharpham* p. 13 mentions that 'above the octagon drawing room there are two oval bedrooms, with a small oval ante-room at each end.'

4   London houses

1 Walpole, *Anecdotes*, V, p. 194.

2 *Gentleman's Magazine*, 1788, II, p. 1070.

3 *Survey of London*, III, pp. 36–47 and Plates, 24–41. From 1758 Abdy's house, 36, was rated at £130 and Sewell's at £150.

4 ibid. and ratebooks in Holborn Public Library (under 'Portugal Row').

5 *The Builder*, 13 August 1915, p. 117.

6 *Survey of London*, XX, p. 45.

7 *London Chronicle*, LXIV, p. 319.

8 *The Builder*, 24 October 1846.

9 *Survey of London*, XXXIX, fig. 8 (p.121), p. 122; XL, pp.199, 212, 278; fig. 49 (p. 211), Plates 57 and 72a. Taylor witnessed the sale to Sir Henry Houghton in 1769.

10 Namier and Brooke, *House of Commons*, II, pp. 628–9.

11 Ratebooks in Westminster Public Library, Buckingham Palace Road. Miss Dorothy Stroud first drew my attention to this.

12 Grafton Papers in the Suffolk Record Office. See also *Country Life*, 12 and 19 November 1981.

13 Information kindly supplied by Victor Belcher and P. A. Bezodis of the *Survey of London*.

14 Ratebooks in Westminster Public Library, Buckingham Palace Road.

15 Suffolk Record Office, Grafton Papers.

16 Plans and elevations of No. 1 Grafton Street, made in 1899 shortly before demolition, are preserved in the collections of the Greater London Council Historic Buildings Division.
17 Information from Rev. Eric T. Cook and Mrs Olga Clark (later from notes made for Helena Rubenstein the former occupants).
18 See H. R. Steele *The Old Bank of England*, 1930; plate LIV (right) showing the entrance hall of the Court Room Suite.
19 From 1772–74 Lord Villiers is entered at £100, suggesting the house may have been partially complete. Lord Howe's and Sir George Warren's were the only other houses at £210.
20 Basil Boothroyd, *No. 4 Grafton Street*, privately printed n.d. Complete Peerage VII, 90.
21 Grafton Papers in Suffolk Record Office.
22 Christopher Hussey, *The Story of Ely House*, 1953.
23 Gunnis, *Dictionary*, p. 382.
24 *DNB*.
25 Romney Sedgwick, *House of Commons*, II, pp. 184–5.
26 Pevsner, *London*, 1973, I, p. 631.
27 *Survey of London*, XIII, pp. 153–5, Plates 60–3.

5   Public works

1 See the author in *Country Life*, 16 November 1978. Contract and other documents are in the Corporation of London Record Office.
2 Walpole, *Anecdotes*, V, p. 194. Calonne was Comptroller General of Finance in France until 1787.
3 See the author in *Country Life*, 13 and 20 November 1969. H. R. Steele and F. R. Yerbury, *The Old Bank of England*, 1930. W. Marston Acres, *The Bank of England from within 1694–1900*, two volumes, 1931. Original accounts and other documents are at the Bank of England.
4 See David Watkin, *C. R. Cockerell*, 1974, p. 61.
5 Volume X (1847) 340.
6 See Sir Nikolaus Pevsner *A History of Building Types*, 1976, p. 199–201.
7 Quoted in David Watkin *C. R. Cockerell*, 1974, p. 61.
8 Volume X, 1847, p. 340.
9 *Records of the Society of Lincoln's Inn: the Black Books*, III, pp. 407, 410, 412, 423; IV, pp. 5–9, 17, 219, 226.
10 *Architectural Review*, June 1917.
11 Walpole, *Anecdotes*, V, p. 194.
12 *Records of the Society of Lincoln's Inn: the Black Books*, III, pp. 423–4.
13 See Dorothy Stroud, *George Dance, Architect*, 1971, p. 52, and minute books of the committee set up to supervise the alterations and associated bills and proposals in the City of London Record Office. One of 14 alcoves that Dance and Taylor erected along the bridge survives in the inner quadrangle at Guy's Hospital, London. It was acquired in 1861 as a shelter for convalescing patients.
14 Drawings and Borough Sessions Book in Berkshire County Record Office.

15 See Hasted's *Kent*, III, p. 142; Neale's *Seats*, 2nd Series, II; and a faculty granted 24 October 1754 in a registration book in the Diocesan Registry, Canterbury. Information from D. M. M. Carey.

16 Manuscript vestry minutes and other documents in Berkshire County Record Office, D/P 139/6/2–3. Taylor's design is still rococo in spirit.

17 Taylor's designs are preserved in the Surrey Archdeaconry Records, now at the GLC Record Office, DWOP 1778/5 and 1885/3.

18 See J. Britton, *Beauties of Wiltshire* 1801, 87–9.

19 It is probable these domes were modified in execution by Pilkington. One small side lit dome still existed in 1966.

20 *Survey of London*, XVI, pp. 35–9, 145–57.

6   Great houses

1 *Complete Peerage*; Romney Sedgwick, *House of Commons*, II, 87 Namier and Brooke, *House of Commons*, II, 556–7.

2 J. C. Rogers 'The manor and houses of Gorhambury' *St Albans and Hertfordshire Archaeological Society Transactions* 1933; Norah King *The Grimstons of Gorhambury*, 1983.

3 Sir John Summerson 'The Classical Country House in 18th-century England' *Journal of the Royal Society of Arts*, July 1959.

4 *Complete Baronetage; Complete Peerage* (under Huntingfield); Namier and Brooke, *House of Commons* III, 573–4.

5 Jean Marchand (ed.) *A Frenchman in England* 1933, 185–91.

6 Quoted in Alfred Suckling *History of Suffolk* 1848, 390.

Conclusion

1 Walpole, *Anecdotes*, v. 197.

2 Walpole, *Anecdotes*, v. 192.

Bibliography

This bibliography should be read in conjunction with the footnotes which provide references to sources on individual commissions.

The architectural designs of Sir Robert Taylor drawn and executed in aquatint by Thomas Malton 1792. A set of these plates can be found at Sir John Soane's Museum. The Courtauld Institute of Art have negatives from which photographs can be obtained. The Ashmolean holds a number of Malton's drawings, the interior of the Transfer Office (exhibited Royal Academy, 1790); interior of the Reduced Annunity Office; the front of the Bank of England (RA 1789) and the interior court at the Bank (RA 1789); the Rotunda (RA 1790); the entrance front and hall at Heveningham (RA 1790); Maidenhead Bridge; the Exchange, Belfast; Danson; the hall at Purbrook (RA 1791), Asgill House (RA 1791); Gorhambury (RA 1789); Long Ditton Church (RA 1790).

A large volume of Taylor's designs for monuments is in the library of the Taylor Institution at Oxford, with a smaller one containing 12 designs for rococo chimneypieces and overmantels, and a third entitled *Problems in Geometry and Mensuration with Diagrams.* Some 70 architectural books from Taylor's library came to light at the Taylorian about 1970: See *Books from the Library of Sir Robert Taylor in the Library of the Taylor Institution Oxford*, a checklist compiled by D. J. Gilson, 1973. Other Taylor drawings include: a sketch for the window wall of the Court Room at the Bank of England (c 1765), preserved among the archives at the Bank; drawings for Maidenhead Bridge in Berkshire Record Office MAB 4; a plan in the Ashmolean Museum showing Taylor's original scheme for Stone Buildings, Lincoln's Inn c1774; a drawing for the tower and spire of St Peter's Wallingford 1776–77 in the Berkshire Record Office, D/P 139/6/2–3; drawings for Long Ditton Church, Surrey, 1778 GLC Record Office DWOP/1885/3; a drawing of the proposed dining room at Trewithen, Cornwall, Cornwall County Record Office, Hawkins papers, see *Country Life* April 2 and 9, 1953; a small number of Taylor's drawings have recently appeared among a group of Strickland-Freeman drawings, associated with the Freemans of Chute Lodge and Fawley Court, and are to be auctioned at Christies in the autumn of 1983.

Horace Walpole *Anecdotes of Painting* ed. Hilles & Daghlian, 1937, 190–200, which largely repeats the obituary in the *Gentleman's Magazine*, 1788 (ii) 842, 1930. A slightly extended version is printed in the *London Magazine* lxiv, 1788, September 27–30, 319.

The Farington Diary May 20, 1797; August 20, 1807; November 5, 1821
Walpole Society *Vertue Note Books* 11, 161

The Builder, November 24, 1846, 505

The Civil Engineer and Architect's Journal, x, 1847, 340

B. Ferrey *Recollections of A.W.N. Pugin*, 1861.

Marcus Binney 'The Villas of Sir Robert Taylor' *Country Life* 6 and 13 July, 1967

Marcus Binney 'Sir Robert Taylor's Bank of England' *Country Life* 13 and 20, November, 1967

Marcus Binney 'The Lord Mayor's Coach' *Country Life* 16 November 1978.

Marcus Binney 'Sir Robert Taylor's Grafton Street' *Country Life* 12 and 19 November, 1981.

H.M. Colvin *Dictionary of British Architects, 1600–1840*, 1978.

Country Life (see annual cumulative index of country houses and gardens)

The Dictionary of Architecture (APSD) ed. Wyatt Papworth for the Architectural Publication Society, 8 vols., 1852–92

Dictionary of National Biography (DNB) (for Taylor and his patrons)

K. A. Esdaile 'Sir Robert Taylor as Sculptor' *Architectural Review*, February 1948 p. 63.

Rupert Gunnis *Dictionary of British Sculptors 1660–1851*

The History of Parliament: Romney Sedgwick *The House of Commons 1715–1754*; Sir Lewis Namier and John Brooke *The House of Commons 1754–90*, 1964 (for Taylor's clients)

A. E. Richardson and C. L. Gill *London Houses from 1660 to 1820*, 1911

Sir John Summerson *Architecture in Britain 1530–1830*, 1953 and later editions

Sir John Summerson *Georgian London*, 1945 and later editions.

Index

PLATES

1.   Portrait of Sir Robert Taylor at the Royal Institute of British Architects. Unsigned but, on the evidence of an engraving in the British Museum, by William Miller.

2. Principal front of the first design for Gorhambury, Hertfordshire, built for the 3rd Viscount Grimston 1777–90 (Malton). The windows were to be without architraves.

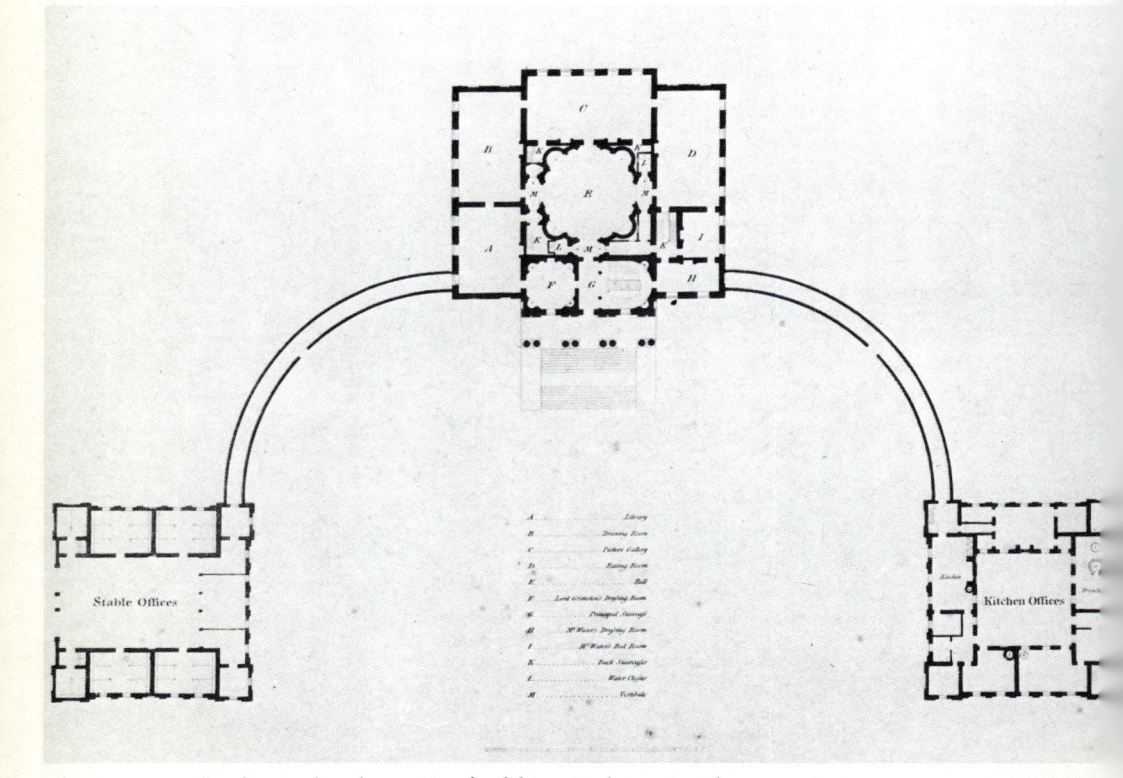

3. First plan for Gorhambury, Hertfordshire (Malton). A, Library; B, Drawing Room; C, Picture Gallery; D, Eating Room; E, Hall; F, Lord Grimston's Dressing Room; H, Mr Walter's Dressing Room; I, Mr Walter's Bedroom.

4. Gorhambury as executed.

5. Heveningham Hall, Suffolk, c 1777–80. Built for Sir Gerard Vanneck. The house from across the Capability Brown lake.

6. The centrepiece of the entrance front at Heveningham. The powerful attic and free standing columns anticipate Nash's terraces in Regent's Park.

7. 70 Lombard Street. Banking house built for Sir Charles Asgill, Bt, c 1756, (Malton). The ground floor has the bold vermiculated rustication which is a hallmark of Taylor's work.

8. The Bank by William Marlow. Taylor also designed the triangular block in the centre known as Bank Buildings (1764–66). This was praised for its ingenious use of a difficult site but demolished in 1844.

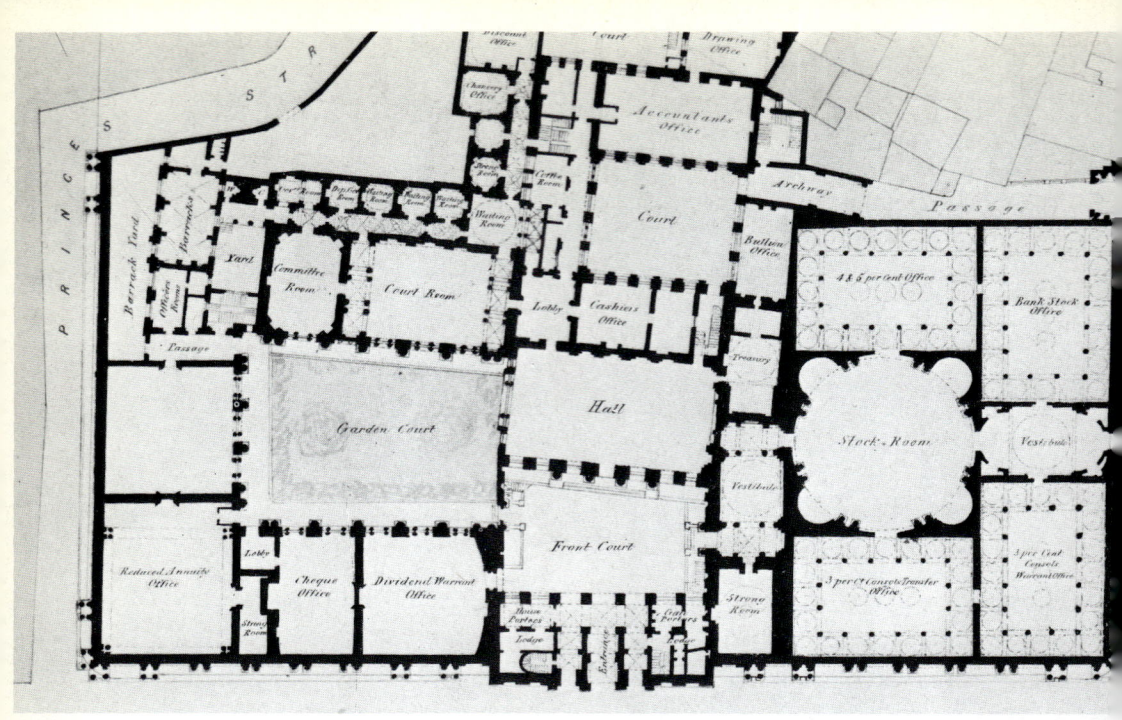

9. Plan of the Bank of England at Taylor's death in 1788. On the right are the rotunda and transfer offices he added in 1765–68; on left, across the Garden Court, the Court Room and associated offices built 1765–70 and on Threadneedle Street the Reduced Annuity Office completed in 1787.

10. The Rotunda, or Brokers' Exchange, at the Bank of England (Malton). Modelled on the Pantheon in Rome but the prototype for covered exchanges all over Britain in the nineteenth century.

11. View of one of the four Transfer Offices (Malton). An ambitious experiment in top-lighting.

12. Taylor's proposal for the Court Room c. 1765. There are still elements of rococo decoration in the arches around the windows which Taylor decided to glaze.

13. View of the Court Room at the Bank in 1929. C. R. Cockerell writing in 1845 noted Taylor's frequent use of arcades at the end of a room allowing its proportions to be 'enjoyed as it were from an external point of view.'

14. Plasterwork in one of the arcades of the Court Room (photograph taken shortly before dismantling in 1929).

15. The West Quadrangle at the Bank with the Court Room on the right (Malton). Taylor greatly increased the light by glazing in the outer arch of the Venetian windows.

16. The Reduced Annuity Office at the Bank completed in 1787 (Malton). Taylor here introduced the shallow side-lit domes which were to be such a hallmark of his successor as architect to the Bank, Sir John Soane.

17. Maidenhead Bridge, Berkshire, 1772–77 (Malton). An instance of Taylor's lifelong penchant for vermiculated rustication around arches.

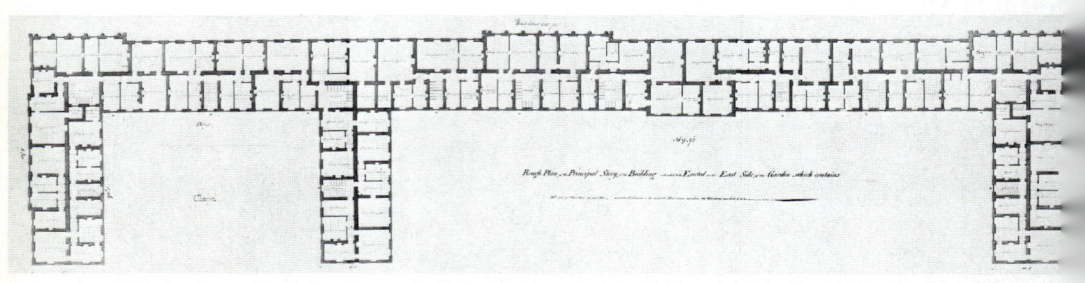

18. Original proposal for Stone Buildings, Lincoln's Inn, London, built 1774–80. This shows Taylor originally intended a projecting centre as well as projecting end pavilion.

19. The west front of Stone Buildings. The south pavilion was completed in 1842–45 by P. Hardwick.

20. The Six Clerks' and Enrolment Office at Lincoln's Inn, 1775–77. Here Taylor dispenses with an order giving the building a more neo-classical look.

21. The executed, classical design for Long Ditton Church, Surrey, begun 1778. Demolished 1880 (Malton).

22. The Gothic spire Taylor added to St. Peter's Wallingford, Berkshire, in 1776–77. Still rococo-gothick in character.

23. The Guildhall, Salisbury, as Taylor intended (Malton). The design, dating from 1788, was considerably modified by Taylor's pupil, W. Pilkington, in execution. A canted bay, and projecting and recessed porticoes created a sense of movement in the elevations.

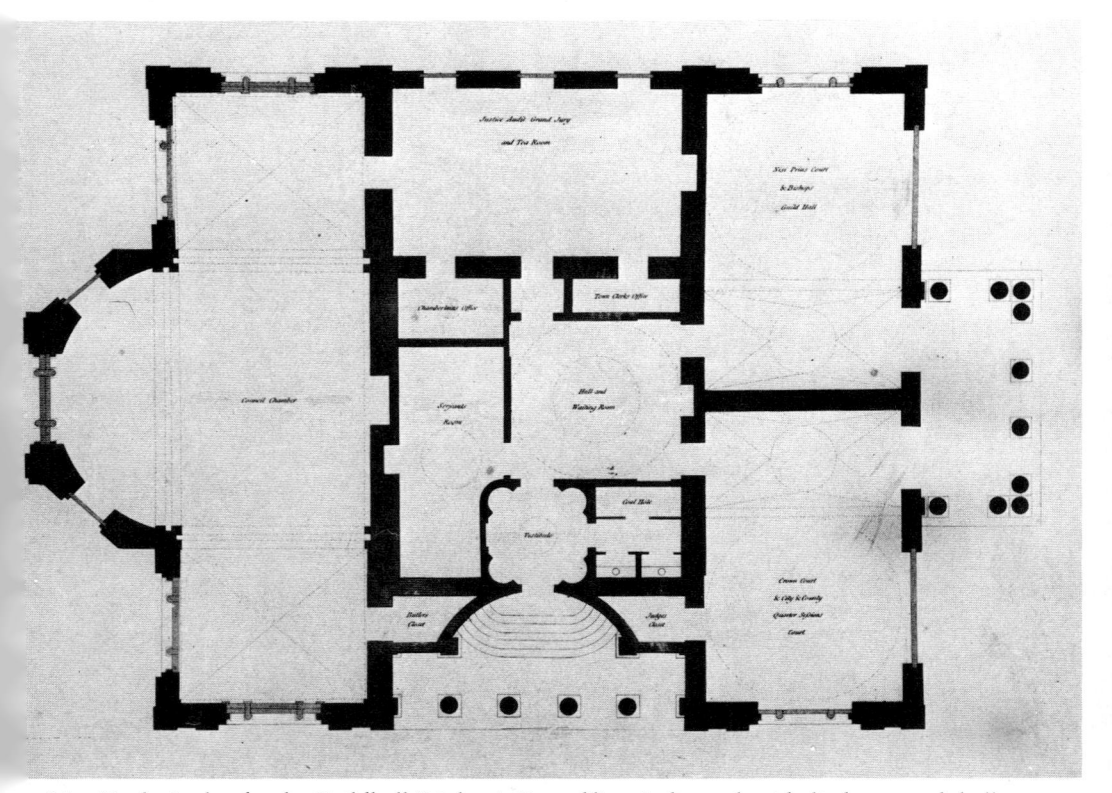

24. Taylor's plan for the Guildhall (Malton). Dotted lines indicate the side-lit domes and shallow cross-vaults Taylor intended.

25. Harleyford Manor, Buckinghamshire. The house stands on the banks of the Thames. The setting is somewhat idealized in this painting attributed to Zuccharelli, but it shows the canted bay at the side with a Diocletian window above before it was raised. The painting is now at Squerryes, Kent.

26. Harleyford Manor, Buckinghamshire, for Sir William Clayton, Bt. The house was under construction in 1755. Note Taylor's characteristic octagonal glazing in the window on the right.

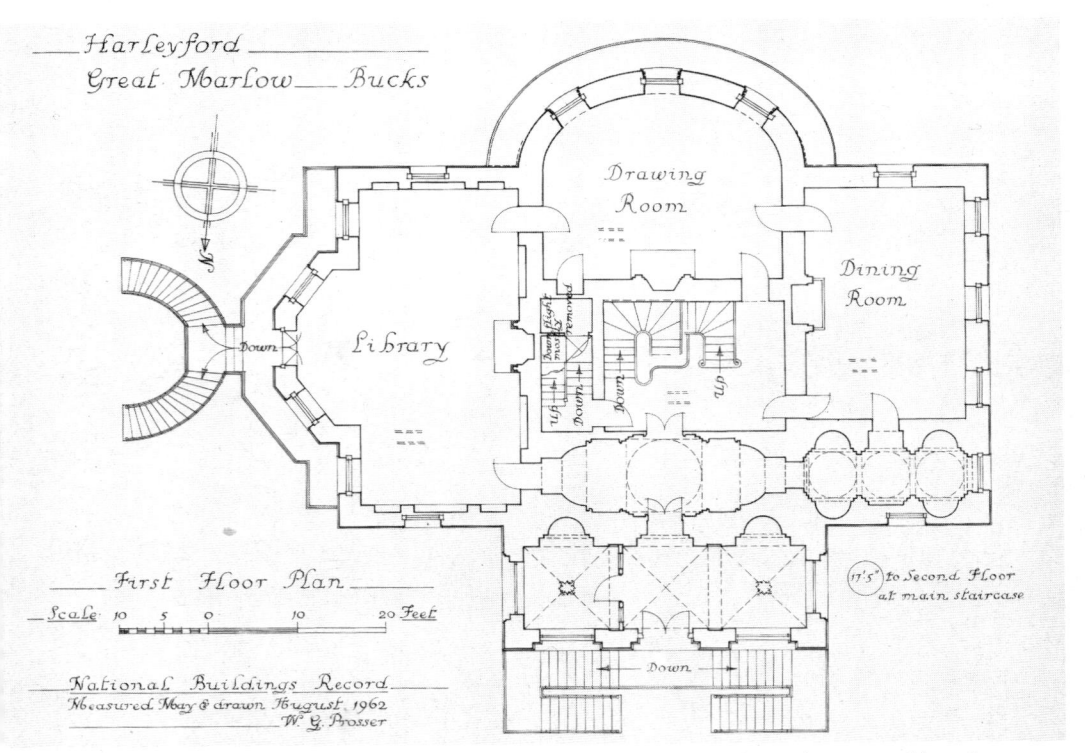

27. Plan of the first floor at Harleyford. The domed corridor on the right is possibly a later addition.

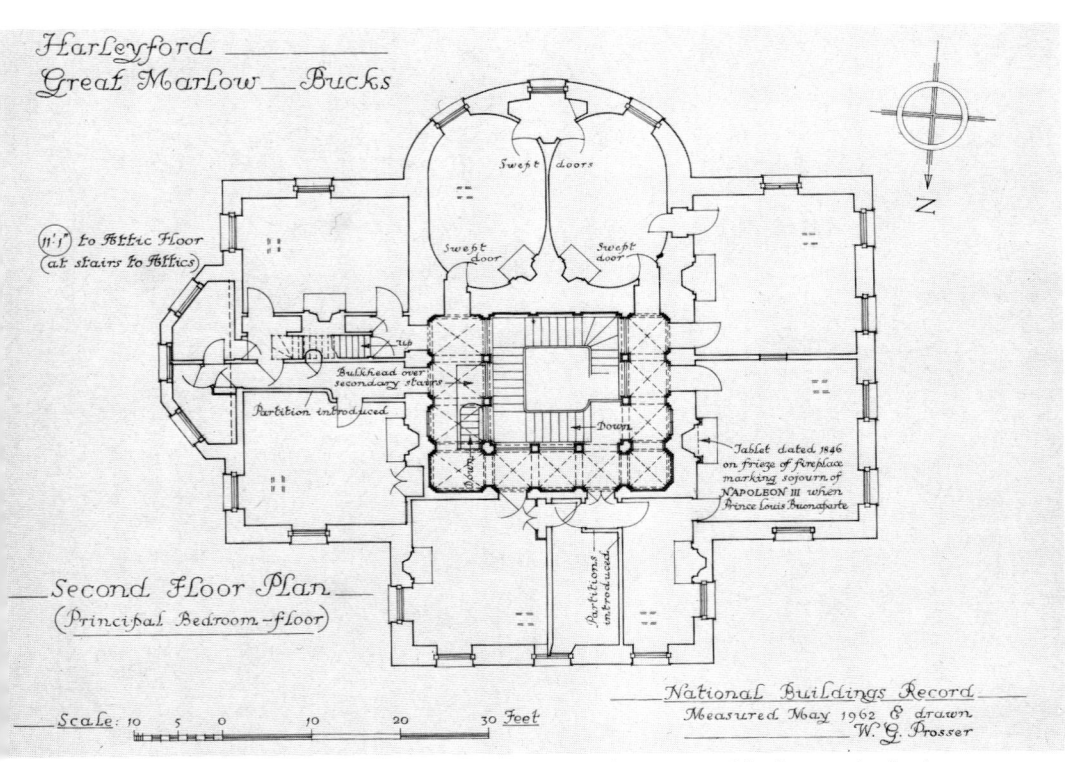

28. Plan of the second floor at Harleyford. Note the twin oval bedrooms in the bow.

29. The Saloon at Harleyford in 1910. Octagonal door panels matched the windows.

30. The Library at Harleyford. The shallow arches and roundels above recur frequently in Taylor's work.

31. The staircase at Harleyford. The arcading on the first floor landing and the coved ceiling is almost identical to Barlaston. The stair balustrade has been renewed.

32. Coptfold Hall, Essex, begun in 1755 for Richard Holden, demolished 1850 (Malton). A typical example of Taylor's astylar elevations, of classical proportions but without columns or pilasters. Note the canted bay at the side surmounted by a Venetian window.

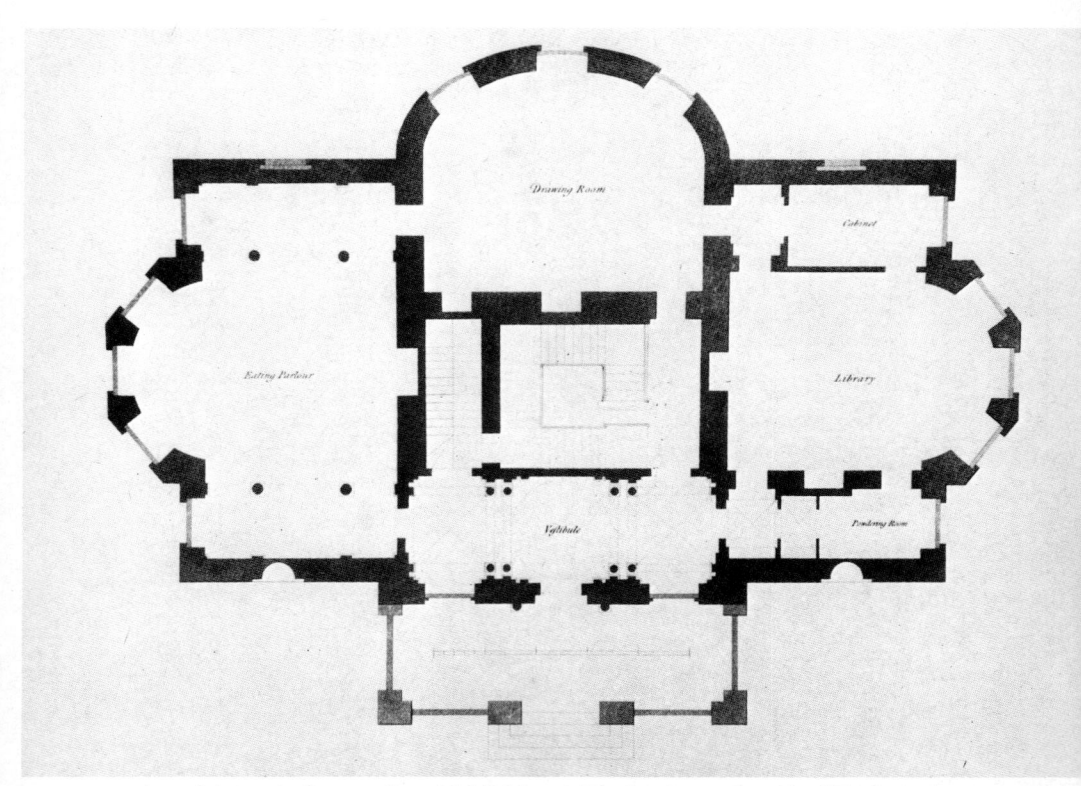

33. Plan of the main floor at Coptfold (Malton). The 'eating parlour' had Taylor's characteristic screens of columns at either end.

34. Barlaston Hall, Staffordshire, under construction in 1756–57, for Thomas Mills. It is strikingly similar in elevation and plan to Coptfold and has Taylor's octagonal glazing.

35. Barlaston from the south-west. All Taylor's 1750s villas make use of powerful elliptical bows and canted bays.

36. The Library before restoration began. The book cases, set into a blind arcade are original and have Taylor's characteristic octagonal glazing.

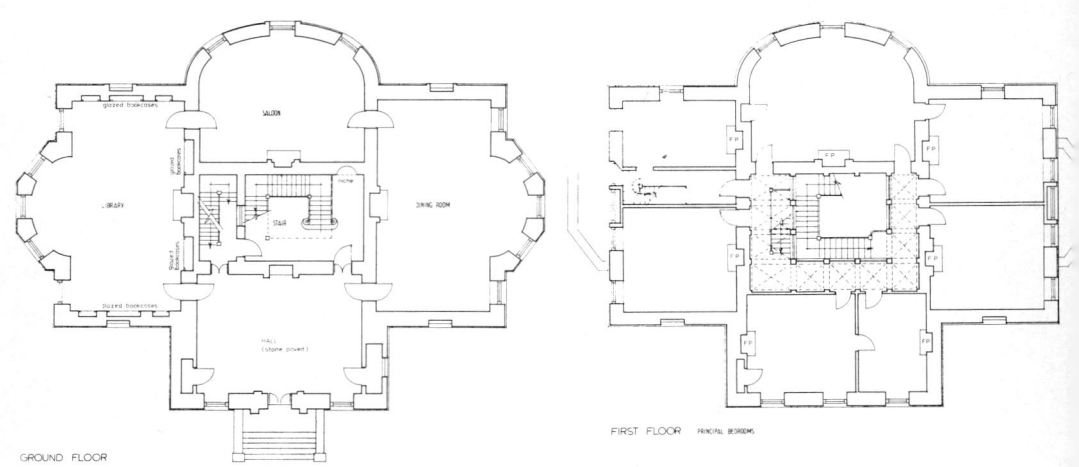

GROUND FLOOR

FIRST FLOOR PRINCIPAL BEDROOMS

37. 2 plans of Barlaston (ground & first floors).

38.   Staircase at Barlaston in 1978. Of wooden cantilever construction with a Chinese Chippendale balustrade. The arcades and coved ceiling are very similar to Harleyford.

39.   Danson Hill, Bexleyheath, Kent, built for Sir John Boyd, Bt, 1762–67 (Malton). The wings were demolished later in the eighteenth century.

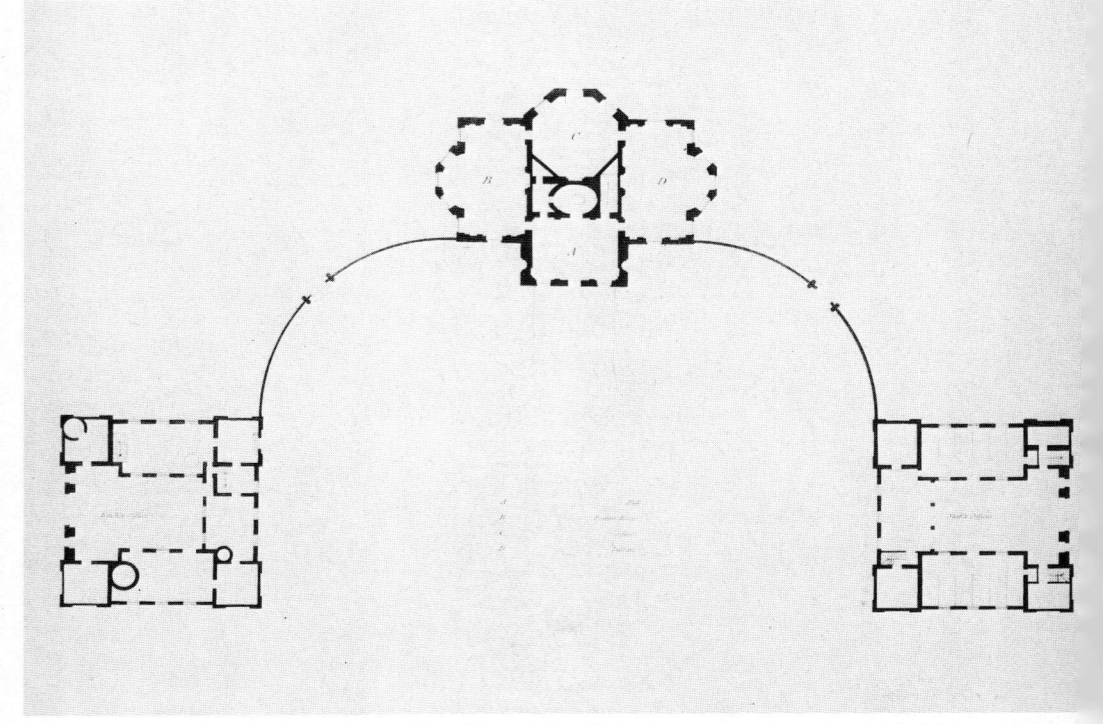

40.   Plan of Danson (Malton). The villas of the 1760s have canted, or three sided, bays on the garden front, not elliptical bows, with octagonal saloons inside.

41. Danson in 1967. The canted bays at the sides have been raised by a storey and the angles of the entrance front filled in with single storey additions.

42. Chute Lodge, Wiltshire. For John Freeman c 1768. A bold example – in red brick – of Taylor's astylar treatment. The canted bays at the side are lower than that on the centre, as Taylor intended. The dormer windows and the wing on the right are later additions.

43. The upper landing at Chute. As at Danson, an oval cantilevered stair is surmounted by a top lit dome resting on a ring of columns.

44. The octagonal saloon at Chute.

45. Asgill House, Richmond, for Sir Charles Asgill, Bt, 1761–64. A novel variant on Palladio's pediment-within-a-pediment motif.

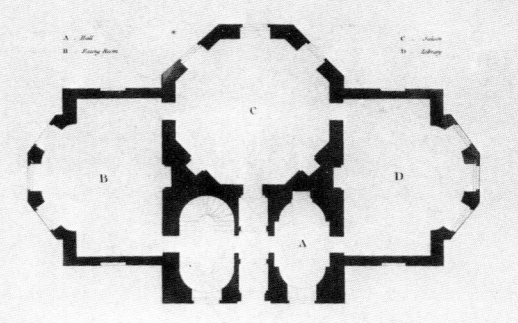

46. Entrance front and plan of the ground floor at Asgill (Malton). Taylor proposed an apsed hall similar to that at 35 Lincoln's Inn Fields (Plate 66) to balance the oval staircase.

47.   View across the first floor landing at Asgill. The stairs to the upper floor rise under the sloping sides of the roof.

48. Ottershaw, Surrey, built for Sir Thomas Sewell soon after 1761 (Prosser). Demolished 1908. Typical of the 1760s villas with a canted bay on the garden front.

49. Purbrook House, Hampshire, for Peter Taylor c 1770 (Malton). Demolished 1829. Though a substantial house it still has the villa's 1–3–1 rhythm of windows and as usual Taylor eschews the use of columns or pilasters, except on the doorcase.

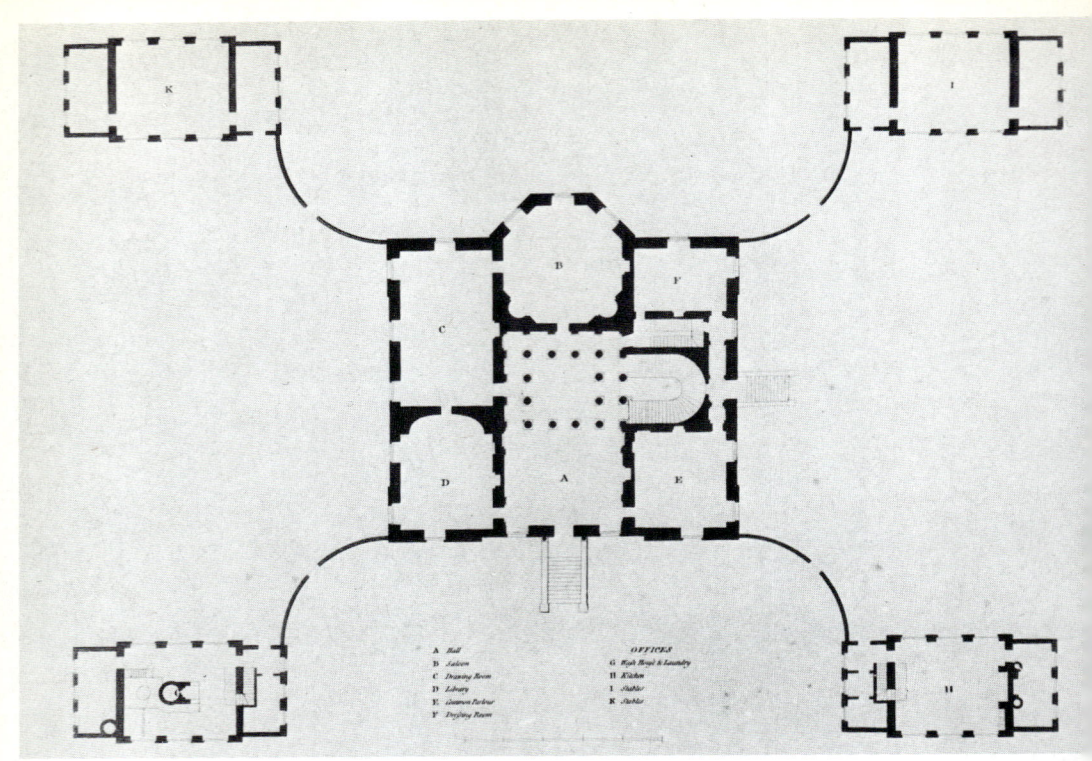

50. Plan of the principal floor of Purbrook (Malton). This shows a new openness in Taylor's planning with no walls or doors between hall, atrium and staircase.

51. The hall at Purbrook (Malton). Certainly the earliest known recreation of a Roman atrium in England probably inspired by contemporary excavations at Herculaneum.

52.   Looking down on Sharpham. Taylor's villas all stand in commanding positions so as to see and be seen, but this is the most spectacular position of all.

53.   The entrance front of Sharpham House, Devon, built for Captain Philemon Pownoll c 1770. Executed in superb ashlar, with ornamental detail pared to minimum, it is already neo-classical in spirit.

54. The entrance hall at Sharpham. Octagonal in shape with a circle of Doric columns and a compass pattern floor inset. A glimpse of the stair beyond is provided through an opening without doors.

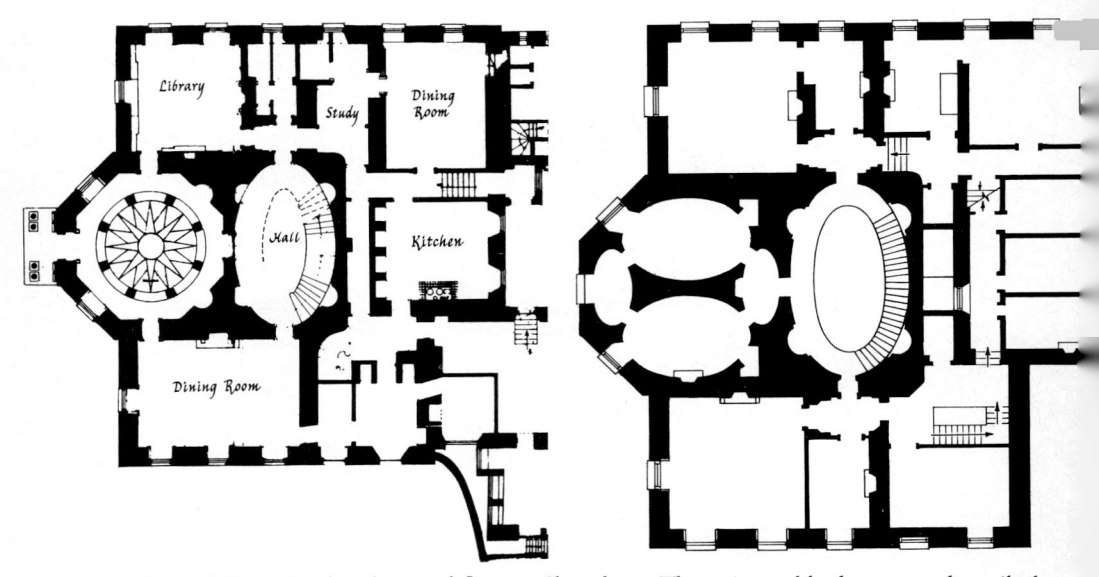

55. Plans of the ground and second floor at Sharpham. The twin oval bedrooms and vestibules on the second floor are here reconstructed as they probably were laid out.

56. The staircase hall at Sharpham. A huge oval cylinder with the dome springing directly from the walls. The stairs and landings are dramatically cantilevered without any additional support from below.

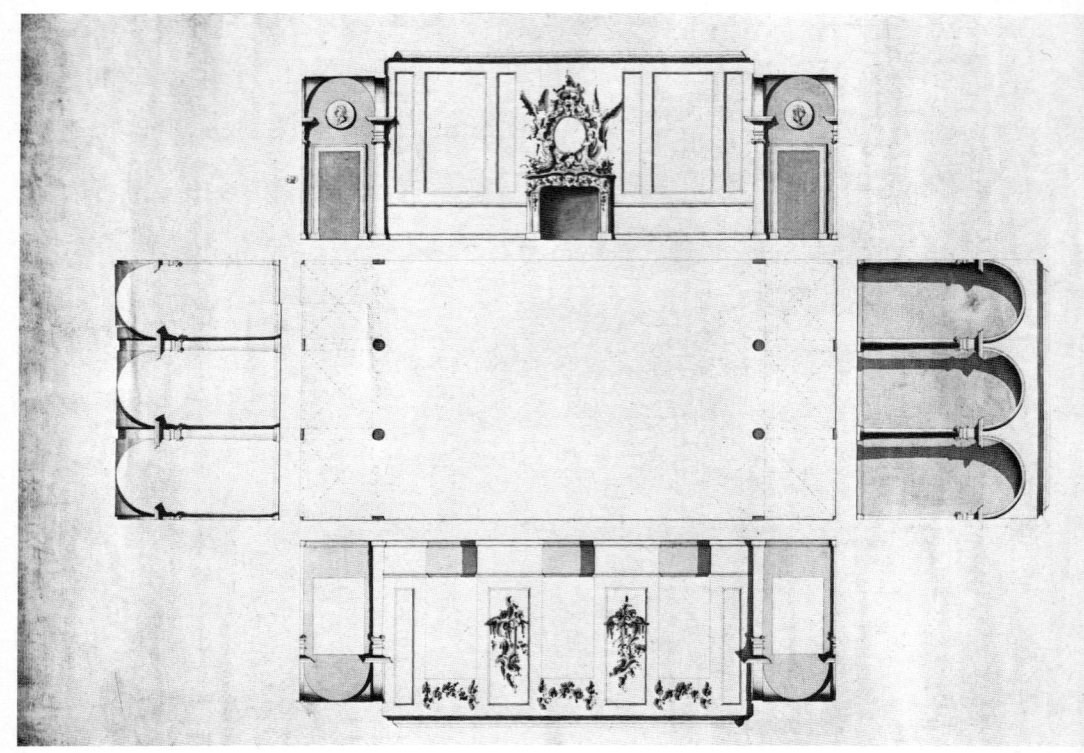

57. Taylor's drawing for the dining room at Trewithen.

58. The dining room at Trewithen, Cornwall, designed for Thomas Hawkins, c 1763–64. This shows Taylor's characteristic arcades at either end and a chimneypiece and overmantel very similar to his designs for chimneypieces.

59–62.   Four of the twelve designs by Taylor in a book of designs for chimneypieces now in the Taylorian Institution at Oxford (c 1750–55).

63. The dining room or ball room at the Oaks, Carshalton, Surrey, added for General John Burgoyne, c 1770, and here attributed to Taylor.

64. 35 Lincoln's Inn Fields, London, completed in 1757 for Sir Charles Sewell. Destroyed in 1941. Built as one of a matching pair, approached by the shared staircase on the right.

65. The rear elevation of 35 Lincoln's Inn Fields, with an unusually monumental, pedimented "back extension". The octagonal glazing is a hallmark of Taylor's work in the 1750s.

66. The hall at 35 Lincoln's Inn Fields. An early example of Taylor's liking for architectural spaces with a dome, blind arches at the sides and a stepped apse at the end.

67. Arched screen in the back room on the first floor of 35 Lincoln's Inn Fields, with barrel vaulted sides and a cross vaulted centre; this is a frequent feature in Taylor's houses.

68. The oval staircase at first floor landing of 35 Lincoln's Inn Fields. The doors had octagonal panels matching the windows.

69. Middle room on the ground floor of 35 Lincoln's Inn Fields. The square and round panels on the upper wells constantly recur in Taylor's work.

70. The Rear Room on the ground floor of 35 Lincoln's Inn Fields. A Venetian arch motif on both wells, with roundels above.

72 (right). View of the entrance vestibule and staircase at 4 Grafton Street completed for Lord Villiers in 1775. Cross vaults and elliptical arches appear increasingly in Taylor's later work.

71. 3–6 Grafton Street, London W1. The only survivors of a group of fourteen houses built here by Taylor from 1768 onwards. Only the height above the ground and first floor windows give an idea of the grandeur within.

73. The staircase at 3 Grafton Street completed for Admiral Lord Howe in 1771. The house was remodelled for Mrs Arthur James early this century.

74. Looking up the staircase well at 4 Grafton Street. With Sharpham, the most dramatic of all Taylor's top lit cantilevered staircases.

75.   The former ballroom at 4 Grafton Street. From the 1770s Taylor made increasing use of classical reliefs as decorative motifs usually in roundels.

76.   Back room on the first floor of 4 Grafton Street. A highly architectural treatment of a small room with elliptical arches supporting a cross vault.

77. 12 Grafton Street completed for the Hon. Mrs Howe, Lord Howe's sister, in 1771. Alternate houses in this part of the street had Taylor's characteristic canted bays.

78. The cross vaulted entrance hall at 12 Grafton Street. The arches are inset as usual, with a guilloche.

79. Malton's engraving of the front of Ely House, 37 Dover Street, London, built for Edmund Keene, Bishop of Ely, in 1772–76. Only the bishop's mitre over the central window proclaims a clerical occupant.

80. Taylor's forceful vermiculated rustication on the ground floor of Ely House.

81. The dome over the top lit staircase at Ely House. Barrel vaults carry the dome at either end.